Letts
gets you through

WJEC Eduqas GCSE 9-1

ENGLISH LANGUAGE AND LITERATURE

PRACTICE TEST PAPERS

PAUL BURNS

Contents

English Language

Component 1: 20th Century Literature Reading and Creative Prose Writing 3

Component 2: 19th and 21st Century Non-fiction Reading and Transactional/Persuasive Writing 8

English Literature

Component 1: Shakespeare and Poetry 15

Component 2: Post-1914 Prose/Drama, 19th Century Prose and Unseen Poetry 29

Answers 48

ACKNOWLEDGEMENTS

The author and publisher are grateful to the copyright holders for permission to use quoted materials and images.

Page 30 From *Lord of the Flies* by William Golding (1954). Reprinted by permission of the publishers, Faber and Faber Ltd.
Page 31 From *Anita and Me* by Meera Syal Reprinted by permission of HarperCollins Publishers Ltd© (1997) (Meera Syal)
Page 32 From *Never Let Me Go* by Kazuo Ishiguro (2010). Reprinted by permission of the publishers, Faber and Faber Ltd.
Page 33 From *The Woman in Black* by Susan Hill (1983).
Page 34 From *Oranges are Not the Only Fruit* by Jeanette Winterson (1985).
Page 35 © Simon Stephens, 2004, The Curious Incident of the Dog in the Night-Time, Methuen Drama, an imprint of Bloomsbury Publishing Plc.
Page 36 © Shelagh Delaney, 1982, A Taste of Honey, Methuen Drama, an imprint of Bloomsbury Publishing Plc.
Page 37 From AN INSPECTOR CALLS by J.B. Priestley (Penguin Books, 2001) Copyright © J.B. Priestley, 1947. Reproduced by permission of Penguin Books Ltd
Page 38 From *The History Boys* by Alan Bennett (2004), Faber and Faber Ltd.
Page 39 © Willy Russell, 2001, Blood Brothers, Methuen Drama, an imprint of Bloomsbury Publishing Plc.
All images are © Shutterstock.com

Every effort has been made to trace copyright holders and obtain their permission for the use of copyright material. The author and publisher will gladly receive information enabling them to rectify any error or omission in subsequent editions. All facts are correct at time of going to press.

Published by Letts Educational
An imprint of HarperCollins*Publishers*
1 London Bridge Street
London SE1 9GF

ISBN: 9780008321727

First published 2019

10 9 8 7 6 5 4 3 2 1

© HarperCollins*Publishers* Limited 2019

All rights reserved. No part of this publication may be reproduced, stored in a retrieval system, or transmitted, in any form or by any means, electronic, mechanical, photocopying, recording or otherwise, without the prior permission of Letts Educational.

British Library Cataloguing in Publication Data.

A CIP record of this book is available from the British Library.

Commissioning Editor: Kerry Ferguson
Author: Paul Burns
Editor and Project Manager: Katie Galloway
Cover Design: Amparo Barrera
Inside Concept Design: Ian Wrigley
Text Design and Layout: Jouve India Private Limited
Production: Karen Nulty
Printed and bound by CPI Group (UK) Ltd, Croydon, CR0 4YY

GCSE ENGLISH LANGUAGE

COMPONENT 1

20th Century Literature Reading and
Creative Prose Writing

1 hour 45 minutes

INSTRUCTIONS TO CANDIDATES

Answer **all** questions in Section A.

Select **one** option to use for your writing in Section B.

Write your answers on separate sheets of paper.

INFORMATION FOR CANDIDATES

You are advised to spend your time as follows:

Section A	– about 10 minutes reading
	– about 50 minutes answering the questions
Section B	– about 10 minutes planning
	– about 35 minutes writing

Section A (Reading): 40 marks

Section B (Writing): 40 marks

The number of marks is given in brackets at the end of each question or part-question.

SECTION A Reading: 40 marks

Read carefully the passage below. Then answer all the questions which follow it.

This extract is the opening of 'Home Sickness', a short story by George Moore, first published in 1903. The story opens in New York.

He told the doctor he was due in the bar-room at eight o'clock in the morning; the bar-room was in a slum in the Bowery; and he had only been able to keep himself in health by getting up at five o'clock and going for long walks in the Central Park.

'A sea voyage is what you want,' said the doctor. 'Why not go to Ireland for two or three months?
5 You will come back a new man.'

'I'd like to see Ireland again.'

And he began to wonder how the people at home were getting on. The doctor was right. He thanked him, and three weeks after he landed in Cork.

As he sat in the railway carriage he recalled his native village, built among the rocks of the large
10 headland stretching out into the winding lake. He could see the houses and the streets, and the fields of the tenants, and the Georgian mansion and the owners of it; he and they had been boys together before he went to America. He remembered the villagers going every morning to the big house to work in the stables, in the garden, in the fields – mowing, reaping, digging, and Michael Malia building a wall; it was all as clear as if it were yesterday, yet he had been thirteen years in
15 America; and when the train stopped at the station, the first thing he did was to look round for any changes that might have come into it. It was the same blue limestone station as it was thirteen years ago, with the same five long miles between it and Duncannon. He had once walked these miles gaily, in a little over an hour, carrying a heavy bundle on a stick, but he did not feel strong enough for the walk today, though the evening tempted him to try it. A car[1] was waiting at the
20 station, and the boy, discerning from his accent and his dress that Bryden had come from America, plied him with questions, which Bryden answered rapidly, for he wanted to hear who were still living in the village, and if there was a house in which he could get a clean lodging. The best house in the village, he was told, was Mike Scully's, who had been away in a situation for many years, as a coachman in the King's County, but had come back and built a fine house with a concrete floor.
25 The boy could recommend the loft, he had slept in it himself, and Mike would be glad to take in a lodger, he had no doubt. Bryden remembered that Mike had been in a situation at the Big House. He had intended to be a jockey, but had suddenly shot up into a fine tall man, and had had to become a coachman instead; and Bryden tried to recall the face, but he could only remember a straight nose, and a somewhat dusky complexion.

30 So Mike had come back from King's County, and had built himself a house, had married – there were children for sure running about; while he, Bryden, had gone to America, but he had come back; perhaps he, too, would build a house in Duncannon, and – his reverie was suddenly interrupted by the carman.

'There's Mike Scully,' he said, pointing with his whip, and Bryden saw a tall, finely-built, middle-
35 aged man coming through the gates, who looked astonished when he was accosted, for he had forgotten Bryden even more completely than Bryden had forgotten him; and many aunts and uncles were mentioned before he began to understand.

'You've grown into a fine man, James,' he said, looking at Bryden's great width of chest. 'But you're thin in the cheeks, and you're very sallow in the cheeks too.'

40 'I haven't been well lately – that is one of the reasons I've come back; but I want to see you all again.'

'And thousand welcome you are.'

Bryden paid the carman, and wished him, 'God speed'. They divided the luggage, Mike carrying the bag and Bryden the bundle, and they walked round the lake, for the townland[2] was at the back of the domain[3]; and while walking he remembered the woods thick and well forested; now they
45 were wind-worn, the drains were choked, and the bridge leading across the lake inlet was falling away. Their way led between long fields where herds of cattle were grazing, the road was broken – Bryden wondered how the villagers drove their carts over it, and Mike told him that the landlord could not keep it in repair, and he would not allow it to be kept in repair out of the rates[4], for then it would be a public road, and he did not think there should be a public road through his property.

50 At the end of many fields they came to the village, and it looked a desolate place, even on this fine evening, and Bryden remarked that the country did not seem to be as much lived in as it used to be. It was at once strange and familiar to see the chickens in the kitchen; and, wishing to re-knit himself to the old customs, he begged of Mrs Scully not to drive them out, saying they reminded him of old times.

55 'And why shouldn't they?' Mike answered, 'he being one of ourselves bred and born in Duncannon, and his father before him.'

'Now, is it the truth ye are telling me?' and she gave him her hand, after wiping it on her apron, telling him he was heartily welcome, only she was afraid he wouldn't care to sleep in the loft.

George Moore

[1]car – here a cab, drawn by a horse, for hire like a taxi
[2]townland – a small area of land – administrative division in Ireland
[3]domain – estate
[4]rates – local taxes

Read lines 1-8.

A1. List **five** things that you learn about Bryden in these lines. [5]

Read lines 9 to 16.

A2. What impressions does the writer create of Duncannon?

You must refer to the language used in the text to support your answer. [5]

Component 1 | English Language | 5

Read lines 16 to 29.

A3. How does the writer describe Bryden's journey from the station and tell the reader about Mike Scully?

You must refer to the language used in the text to support your answer. [10]

Read lines 30 to 41.

A4. How does the writer show the differences between Bryden and Scully and how they react to each other? [10]

You should write about:
- the differences between the two men and how they react to each other
- the writer's use of language and structure to convey these differences and reactions
- the effects on the reader.

You must refer to the text to support your answer.

A5. 'In the last twenty lines or so of this passage, the reader begins to see the reality of life in Duncannon.'

How far do you agree with this view? [10]

You should write about:
- your own thoughts and feelings about how life in Duncannon is presented here and in the passage as a whole
- how the writer has created these thoughts and feelings.

You must refer to the text to support your answer.

SECTION B Writing: 40 marks

In this section you will be assessed for the quality of your creative prose writing skills.

24 marks are awarded for communication and organisation. 16 marks are awarded for vocabulary, sentence structure, spelling and punctuation.

You are advised to spend 45 minutes on this section: about 10 minutes planning and 35 minutes writing.

Aim to write about 450–600 words.

Choose **one** of the following titles for your writing: [40]

EITHER a) Coming Home.

Or, b) After the Accident.

Or, c) Write a story which begins:

'I sat on the park bench and thought about what the doctor had said.'

Or, d) Write a story which ends:

'That was the last time I saw her.'

GCSE ENGLISH LANGUAGE

COMPONENT 2

19th and 21st Century Non-Fiction Reading and Transactional/Persuasive Writing

2 hours

INSTRUCTIONS TO CANDIDATES

Answer **all** questions in Sections A and B.

Write your answers on separate pieces of paper.

INFORMATION FOR CANDIDATES

You are advised to spend your time as follows:

- Section A – about 10 minutes reading
  - about 50 minutes answering the questions
- Section B – spend 30 minutes on each question:
  - about 5 minutes planning
  - about 25 minutes writing

Section A (Reading): 40 marks

Section B (Writing): 40 marks

The number of marks is given in brackets at the end of every question or part-question.

SECTION A Reading: 40 marks

*Answer **all** the following questions.*

The Resource Material for use with Section A is printed on pages 11–12. It is an advertising feature for a local bakery.

The extract on page 13 is from The Food of London *by George Dodd, published in 1856. In this chapter the writer describes how bread is made in London and compares it to what is happening in Paris and Birmingham.*

Read the advertising feature 'Archie's Artisan Bakery'.

A1. (a) Name the city where Archie worked as a sous chef. [1]
     (b) Name the country in which Archie met his wife. [1]
     (c) Give one quality which, according to the writer, a good baker needs. [1]

A2. How does the writer try to persuade the reader to buy his products? [10]

    You should comment on:
- what he says to influence readers
- his use of language and tone.

To answer the following questions you will need to read the extract on page 13 by George Dodd.

A3. (a) What is the profession of M. Payen? [1]
     (b) How does M. Rolland's machine save labour? [1]
     (c) What source of power drives the machinery in the Birmingham factory? [1]

A4. What do you think and feel about George Dodd's views on bread making? [10]

    You should comment on:
- what is said
- how it is said.

You must refer to the text to support your comments.

To answer the following questions you will need to read both texts.

A5. Using information from both texts explain the differences between Lucy's bread mill, as described by George Dodd, and Archie's bakery. [4]

A6. Both of these texts are about bread making.

Compare:
- the writers' attitudes to bread making;
- how they make their views clear to the reader. [10]

You must use the texts to support your comments and make it clear which text you are referring to.

Archie's Artisan Bakery

Welcome!

Here at Archie's Artisan Bakery, we're putting baking back into the heart of the community. Step into our village bakery and you'll be greeted by the smell of freshly baked bread - a smell that says 'home' - and the sight of a dazzling array of breads, pastries and cakes.

Archie and Fab

Hi, I'm Archie Bold, the co-owner of Archie's Artisan Bakery and the master baker. I'm a local lad, coming from a long line of bakers and confectioners. After attending a local catering college and spending a year as a sous chef at a Michelin starred London restaurant, I felt the family trade calling. But I was also aware of how many of the traditional skills have been lost here in Britain. To get the best possible training, I took myself off to France, where I trained with some of the world's best artisan bakers.

I also fell in love, not just with French baking but with *maîtresse patissiere*, 'Fab' Fabienne Rollard. Five years later we're married and I've fulfilled my childhood dream by opening my own bakery in the beautiful village of Rotterthwaite, just ten miles from my hometown.

Today, Fab's fabulous choux pastry creations bring a touch of Parisian sophistication to our village bakery, sitting happily alongside more traditional British cakes, many inspired by old family recipes.

Real Bread!

What do we mean by real bread? Well, we don't mean white sliced pre-packaged bread, full of additives and made on an industrial scale in huge factories. Nor do we mean the bread that you might find in your local supermarket, supposedly 'baked on the premises' when in fact it has been half-baked somewhere else, driven miles in a van to your local store and then 'finished off' quickly.

Real bread - or artisan bread as it's often called - is made with just four things: flour, water, salt and yeast.

In France, a shop can only call itself a *boulangerie* if all five processes involved in bread making - fermentation, mixing, kneading, shaping and baking - happen in the one place. We don't have that rule in Britain, but that's exactly what happens at Archie's. And it's all done by hand.

I believe that real bread is more than food for the body - it's food for the soul. My assistants, Stan and Rita, and I bring years of experience and expertise to our craft. We also bring passion and love. A real baker bakes not just with the head and the hands, but with the heart.

How We Make Our Bread

For us, local ingredients are key. We source our ingredients locally wherever possible. Our top quality organic flour, for example, comes from Gorton's Mills just thirty miles down the road. The bread-making process starts with 'starter', created from flour and water and natural yeast - wild yeasts for our increasingly popular sourdough range.

A good loaf takes many hours to create. And a good baker needs patience as well as skill and flair.

After we've shaped our loaves and allowed them to gently rise, they are baked in our traditional oven.

In this way, we can produce over 200 top-quality loaves of the finest artisan breads each day - sourdoughs, baguettes, wholemeal, crusty white, granary and even gluten-free.

Visit Us!

We are open from Monday to Saturday between 8.30 a.m. and 5.00 p.m. and you're welcome to visit and see us at work whenever the shop is open. We'll even show you round the bakery and share some of our secrets.

We also have a local delivery service and you can order your bread and cakes the day before you want them, either online, by telephone or just by popping into the shop. Keep in touch with us via our website where you'll find full details (and mouth-watering pictures!) of all our delicious products.

from The Food of London

The bread-making processes are, indeed, clumsily managed in the majority of London establishments. Whoever has seen the rude and primitive mode in which dough is kneaded, by a man straddling and wriggling on the end of a lever or pole, may well marvel that such uncouthness should not long ago have been superseded by something better. Our Parisian neighbours appear
5 to be somewhat in the same plight as ourselves. On a recent occasion, M. Payen, a distinguished French chemist, made a report to the Académie Française on the bread and baking of Paris. He said: "A day will doubtless come when our descendants, who shall read the technology of the 19th century, will ask themselves whether at this time of industrial progress we really prepared the chief of our aliments by the rude way which we now witness — in plunging the arms into the
10 dough, lifting it up and crushing it down with such effort as to exhaust the energy of the half-naked arms, and make the perspiration run down into the food; whether at such an epoch the baking was effected on the very hearth itself from whence the fuel had just been withdrawn; whether it could be believed that during these fatiguing operations the chief part of the heat should seem destined to heat, or rather to roast, the workmen, than to bake the bread!" The Parisian practice is
15 tolerably well marked out in this passage; but improvements seem to be in progress. A committee of the Academie, MM. Payen, Poncelet, and Boussingault, have reported in high terms on a system invented and patented by M. Rolland, in which a kneading machine, worked by hand, will knead a sack of flour into dough in 20 minutes, with a vast saving of muscular labour.

It is strange that, in the greatest city in the world, we have nothing that can be called a large bread-
20 factory. Steam-mills there are on a gigantic scale, as has already been noticed; biscuit-bakeries, in which steam-power is employed to mix and knead the dough; bakers who make frequent changes and improvements in their ovens; but no establishment wherein the plain familiar four pound loaf is made by machinery.

[…]There are now six large bread mills in Birmingham…At one of the largest of these mills,
25 belonging to Mr Lucy, lately Mayor of Birmingham, steam-worked cranes haul up the sacks of wheat from a canal of granaries at the top of the building; steam works fourteen pairs of millstones to grind the corn; steam mixes the wheat before grinding, and the flour after grinding; steam kneads the flour, and water, and yeast, and salt into well-made dough; and then comes the manipulative processes. The bakehouse has tables of large size, and around its walls are eight
30 ovens of great capacity. The dough is made into loaves; the loaves are nicely baked in the ovens; and the baked bread is placed on shelves in a storeroom which will contain 2000 loaves. The mill sells flour as well as bread. At an early hour in the mornings waggons draw up to the mill; they are filled with loaves, which are quickly conveyed to the several hucksters' shops, and the waggoner, or attendant servant, returns with the ready money. The huckster sells the bread to the families of
35 the working men of Birmingham.

George Dodd

SECTION B Writing: 40 marks

Answer questions B1 and B2.

In this section you will be assessed for the quality of your writing skills.

For each question 12 marks are awarded for communication and organisation; 8 marks are awarded for vocabulary, sentence structure, spelling and punctuation.

Think about the purpose and audience of your writing.

You should aim to write about 300–400 words for each task.

B1. The local council has announced that from next term all local students and pupils will be stopped from bringing 'unhealthy' food, such as crisps and sweets, into schools and colleges.

Write a letter to your local newspaper giving your views. [20]

B2. Your school is having a 'Dragons' Den' style competition for young entrepreneurs with ideas for new businesses. Your group has decided to open a restaurant and has chosen you to give a speech to the judges about your project.

Write your speech.

You could include:
- details of your project
- an explanation of why you have chosen it and why the judges should support it. [20]

GCSE ENGLISH LITERATURE

COMPONENT 1

Shakespeare and Poetry

2 hours

SECTION A

Question		Page
1.	*Romeo and Juliet*	16
2.	*Macbeth*	18
3.	*Othello*	20
4.	*Much Ado About Nothing*	22
5.	*Henry V*	24
6.	*The Merchant of Venice*	26

SECTION B

| 7. | **Poetry** | 28 |

INSTRUCTIONS TO CANDIDATES

Answer **two** questions, **one** from Section A (questions 1–6), **and** Section B (question 7).

Write your answers on separate sheets of paper.

Use of a dictionary is not allowed.

INFORMATION FOR CANDIDATES

Each section carries 40 marks.

You are advised to spend your time as follows:

    Section A – about one hour

    Section B – about one hour

The number of marks is given in brackets at the end of each question or part-question.

5 marks are allocated for accuracy in spelling, punctuation and the use of vocabulary and sentence structures in Section A, question (b).

SECTION A Shakespeare

*Answer on **one** text only.*

1. **Romeo and Juliet**

    *Answer **both** part (a) **and** part (b).*

    You are advised to spend about 20 minutes on part (a), and about 40 minutes on part (b).

    (a)   Read the extract on the opposite page.

    Look at how Friar Laurence and Romeo speak and behave here. What does it reveal to the audience about their relationship? Refer closely to the extract to support your answer. [15]

    (b)   *Write about how Shakespeare presents the connection between love and death in *Romeo and Juliet*. [25]

    *5 of this question's marks are allocated for accuracy in spelling, punctuation and the use of vocabulary and sentence structures.

FRIAR LAURENCE Holy Saint Francis, what a change is here!
Is Rosaline, that thou didst love so dear,
So soon forsaken? Young men's love, then, lies
Not truly in their hearts, but in their eyes.
Jesu Maria, what a deal of brine
Hath washed thy sallow cheeks for Rosaline!
How much salt water thrown away in waste,
To season love, that of it doth not taste!
The sun not yet thy sighs from heaven clears,
Thy old groans yet ring in mine ancient ears;
Lo, here upon thy cheek the stain doth sit
Of an old tear that is not washed off yet.
If e'er thou wast thyself, and these woes thine,
Thou and these woes were all for Rosaline.
And art thou changed? Pronounce this sentence then:
Women may fall, when there's no strength in men.

ROMEO Thou chid'st me oft for loving Rosaline.

FRIAR LAURENCE For doting, not for loving, pupil mine.

ROMEO And bad'st me bury love.

FRIAR LAURENCE Not in a grave
To lay one in, another out to have.

ROMEO I pray thee chide me not. Her I love now
Doth grace for grace and love for love allow;
The other did not so.

FRIAR LAURENCE O, she knew well
Thy love did read by rote that could not spell.
But come, young waverer, come go with me,
In one respect I'll thy assistant be;
For this alliance may so happy prove
To turn your households' rancour to pure love.

2. **Macbeth**

*Answer **both** part (a) **and** part (b).*

You are advised to spend about 20 minutes on part (a), and about 40 minutes on part (b).

(a) Read the extract on the opposite page.

What does this extract show the audience about Macduff and his state of mind at this point in the play? Refer closely to the extract to support your answer. [15]

(b) *Write about how Macbeth changes from loyal subject to ruthless tyrant during the course of the play. [25]

*5 of this question's marks are allocated for accuracy in spelling, punctuation and the use of vocabulary and sentence structures.

MALCOLM   Be comforted.
Let's make us medicines of our great revenge
To cure this deadly grief.

MACDUFF   He has no children. All my pretty ones?
Did you say all? O hell-kite! All?
What, all my pretty chickens and their dam
At one fell swoop?

MALCOLM   Dispute it like a man.

MACDUFF   I shall do so,
But I must also feel it as a man.
I cannot but remember such things were
That were most precious to me. Did heaven look on
And would not take their part? Sinful Macduff,
They were all struck for thee. Naught that I am,
Not for their own demerits but for mine
Fell slaughter on their souls. Heaven rest them now.

MALCOLM   Be this the whetstone of your sword. Let grief
Convert to anger: blunt not the heart, enrage it.

MACDUFF   O, I could play the woman with mine eyes
And braggart with my tongue! But gentle heavens
Cut short all intermission. Front to front
Bring thou this fiend of Scotland and myself.
Within my sword's length set him. If he 'scape,
Heaven forgive him too.

3. **Othello**

   Answer **both** part (a) **and** part (b).

   You are advised to spend about 20 minutes on part (a), and about 40 minutes on part (b).

   (a) Read the extract on the opposite page.

   Look at how Iago speaks and acts here. How would an audience respond to this part of the play? Refer closely to the extract to support your answer. [15]

   (b) *Write about how Shakespeare presents ideas about marriage at different points in the play. [25]

   *5 of this question's marks are allocated for accuracy in spelling, punctuation and the use of vocabulary and sentence structures.

IAGO   That Cassio loves her, I do well believe it.
That she loves him, 'tis apt and of great credit:
The Moor, howbe't that I endure him not,
Is of a constant, loving, noble nature;
And I dare think, he'll prove to Desdemona
A most dear husband: now I do love her too,
Not out of absolute lust (though peradventure
I stand accountant for as great a sin)
But partly led to diet my revenge,
For that I do suspect the lustful Moor
Hath leap'd into my seat, the thought whereof
Doth like a poisonous mineral gnaw my inwards,
And nothing can, nor shall content my soul,
Till I am even with him, wife, for wife:
Or failing so, yet that I put the Moor,
At least, into a jealousy so strong,
That judgement cannot cure; which thing to do,
If this poor trash of Venice, whom I trace
For his quick hunting, stand the putting on,
I'll have our Michael Cassio on the hip,
Abuse him to the Moor, in the rank garb
(For I fear Cassio with my night-cap too)
Make the Moor thank me, love me, and reward me,
For making him egregiously an ass,
And practising upon his peace and quiet,
Even to madness: 'tis here, but yet confused;
Knavery's plain face is never seen, till used.

4. **Much Ado About Nothing**

   Answer **both** part (a) **and** part (b).

   You are advised to spend about 20 minutes on part (a), and about 40 minutes on part (b).

   (a) Read the extract on the opposite page.

   Look at how Don John speaks and acts here. What does it reveal about his character and state of mind at this point in the play? Refer closely to the extract to support your answer. [15]

   (b) *Write about how Shakespeare presents ideas about trickery and deception at different points in the play. [25]

   *5 of this question's marks are allocated for accuracy in spelling, punctuation and the use of vocabulary and sentence structures.

DON JOHN […] I cannot hide what I am. I must be sad when I have a cause, and smile at no man's jests; eat when I have stomach, and
wait for no man's leisure; sleep when I am drowsy, and tend
on no man's business; laugh when I am merry, and claw no
man in his humour.

CONRAD Yea, but you must not make the full show of this till you may do it without controlment. You have of late stood out against your brother, and he hath ta'en you newly into his grace, where it is impossible you should take true root but by the fair weather that you make yourself. It is needful that you frame the season for your own harvest.

DON JOHN I had rather be a canker in a hedge than a rose in his grace, and it better fits my blood to be disdained of all than to fashion a carriage to rob love from any. In this, though I cannot be said to be a flattering honest man, it must not be denied but I am a plain-dealing villain. I am trusted with a muzzle, and enfranchised with a clog. Therefore I have decreed not to sing in my cage. If I had my mouth I would bite. If I had my liberty I would do my liking. In the meantime, let me be that I am, and seek not to alter me.

CONRAD Can you make no use of your discontent?

5. **Henry V**

    Answer **both** part (a) **and** part (b).

    You are advised to spend about 20 minutes on part (a), and about 40 minutes on part (b).

    (a) Read the extract on the opposite page.

    Look at how the Chorus speaks and acts here. How would an audience respond to this part of the play? Refer closely to the extract to support your answer. [15]

    (b) *Write about how Shakespeare presents the effects of war at different points in the play. [25]

    *5 of this question's marks are allocated for accuracy in spelling, punctuation and the use of vocabulary and sentence structures.

CHORUS   O for a Muse of fire, that would ascend
The brightest heaven of invention:
A kingdom for a stage, princes to act,
And monarchs to behold the swelling scene.
Then should the warlike Harry, like himself,
Assume the port of Mars, and at his heels,
Leashed in like hounds, should famine, sword, and fire,
Crouch for employment. But pardon, gentles all,
The flat unraised spirits that hath dared
On this unworthy scaffold to bring forth
So great an object. Can this cock-pit hold
The vasty fields of France? Or may we cram
Within this wooden O the very casques
That did affright the air at Agincourt?
O pardon: since a crooked figure may
Attest in little place a million,
And let us, ciphers to this great account,
On your imaginary forces work.
Suppose within the girdle of these walls
Are now confined two mighty monarchies,
Whose high upreared and abutting fronts
The perilous narrow ocean parts asunder.
Piece out our imperfections with your thoughts:
Into a thousand parts divide one man,
And make imaginary puissance.
Think, when we talk of horses, that you see them,
Printing their proud hoofs i'th' receiving earth;
For 'tis your thoughts that now must deck our kings,
Carry them here and there, jumping o'er times,
Turning th'accomplishment of many years
Into an hourglass – for the which supply,
Admit me Chorus to this history,
Who Prologue-like your humble patience pray
Gently to hear, kindly to judge, our play.

6. **The Merchant of Venice**

   Answer **both** part (a) **and** part (b).

   You are advised to spend about 20 minutes on part (a), and about 40 minutes on part (b).

   (a) Read the extract on the opposite page.

   Look at how Portia speaks and acts here. What does this speech show the audience about her feelings in this part of the play? Refer closely to the extract to support your answer. [15]

   (b) *Is Shylock a sympathetic character? Write about how Shakespeare presents Shylock and how an audience would respond to him at different points in the play. [25]

   *5 of this question's marks are allocated for accuracy in spelling, punctuation and the use of vocabulary and sentence structures.

PORTIA I pray you tarry, pause a day or two
Before you hazard, for in choosing wrong
I lose your company; therefore forbear a while.
There's something tells me, but it is not love,
I would not lose you; and you know yourself
Hate counsels not in such a quality.
But lest you should not understand me well –
And yet a maiden hath no tongue but thought –
I would detain you here some month or two
Before you venture for me. I could teach you
How to choose right, but then I am forsworn.
So will I never be. So may you miss me;
But if you do, you'll make me wish a sin,
That I had been forsworn. Beshrew your eyes!
They have o'erlooked me and divided me;
One half of me is yours, the other half yours –
Mine own I would say: but if mine then yours,
And so all yours. O these naughty times
Puts bars between the owners and their rights!
And so though yours, not yours. Prove it so,
Let Fortune go to hell for it, not I.
I speak too long, but 'tis to piece the time,
To eke it, and to draw it out at length,
To stay you from election.

SECTION B Poetry

*Answer **both** part (a) **and** part (b).*

You are advised to spend about 20 minutes on part (a) and about 40 minutes on part (b).

7. (a) Read the poem below, Sonnet 43 by Elizabeth Barrett Browning.

In this poem Barrett Browning explores her feelings of romantic love. Write about the ways in which she presents her feelings in this poem. [15]

(b) Choose **one** other poem from the anthology in which the poet also writes about love.

Compare the presentation of love in your chosen poem to the presentation of love in Sonnet 43. [25]

In your answer to part (b) you should compare:
- the content and structure of the poems – what they are about and how they are organised;
- how the writers create effects, using appropriate terminology where relevant;
- the contexts of the poems, and how these might have influenced the ideas in them.

Sonnet 43 by Elizabeth Barrett Browning

How do I love thee? Let me count the ways!
I love thee to the depth and breadth and height
My soul can reach, when feeling out of sight
For the ends of Being and Ideal Grace.
I love thee to the level of everyday's
Most quiet need, by sun and candlelight
I love thee freely, as men strive for Right,
I love thee purely, as they turn from Praise;
I love thee with the passion, put to use
In my old griefs, and with my childhood's faith:
I love thee with the love I seemed to lose
With my lost Saints, I love thee with the breath,
Smiles, tears, of all my life – and, if God choose,
I shall but love thee better after death.

GCSE ENGLISH LITERATURE

COMPONENT 2
Post-1914 Prose/Drama, 19th Century Prose and Unseen Poetry
2 hours 30 minutes

SECTION A

Question		Page
1.	*Lord of the Flies*	30
2.	*Anita and Me*	31
3.	*Never Let Me Go*	32
4.	*The Woman in Black*	33
5.	*Oranges are not the Only Fruit*	34
6.	*The Curious Incident of the Dog in the Night Time*	35
7.	*A Taste of Honey*	36
8.	*An Inspector Calls*	37
9.	*The History Boys*	38
10.	*Blood Brothers*	39

SECTION B

11.	*A Christmas Carol*	40
12.	*Silas Marner*	41
13.	*Pride and Prejudice*	42
14.	*War of the Worlds*	43
15.	*Jane Eyre*	44
16.	*The Strange Case of Dr Jekyll and Mr Hyde*	45

SECTION C

17.	*Unseen Poetry*	46

INSTRUCTIONS TO CANDIDATES

Answer **one** question in Section A (questions 1–10), **one** question in Section B (questions 11–16), **and** Section C (question 17).

Write your answers on separate sheets of paper.

Use of a dictionary is not allowed.

INSTRUCTIONS TO CANDIDATES

Each section carries 40 marks.

You are advised to spend your time as follows:

Section A – about 45 minutes

Section B – about 45 minutes

Section C – about one hour.

The number of marks is given in brackets at the end of each question or part-question.

5 marks are allocated for accuracy in spelling, punctuation and the use of vocabulary and sentence structures in Section A.

SECTION A Post-1914 Prose/Drama

*Answer on **one** text only.*

1. **Lord of the Flies**

   You are advised to spend about 45 minutes on this question.

   You should use the extract below and your knowledge of the whole novel to answer this question.

   Write about the idea of 'Britishness' and how it is presented throughout the novel.

   In your response you should:
   - refer to the extract and the novel as a whole;
   - show your understanding of characters and events in the novel. [40]

   5 of this question's marks are allocated for accuracy in spelling, punctuation and the use of vocabulary and sentence structures.

   > 'I should have thought,' said the officer as he visualized the search before him, 'I should have thought that a pack of British boys – you're all British aren't you? – would have been able to put up a better show than that – I mean –'
   > 'It was like that at first,' said Ralph, 'before things –'
   > He stopped.
   > 'We were together then –'
   > The officer nodded helpfully.
   > 'I know. Jolly good show. Like the Coral Island.'
   > Ralph looked at him dumbly. For a moment he had a fleeting picture of the strange glamour that had once invested the beaches. But the island was scorched up like dead wood – Simon was dead – and Jack had... The tears began to flow and sobs shook him. He gave himself up to them now for the first time on the island; great, shuddering spasms of grief that seemed to wrench his whole body. His voice rose under the black smoke before the burning wreckage of the island; and infected by that emotion, the other little boys began to shake and sob too. And in the middle of them, with filthy body, matted hair, and unwiped nose, Ralph wept for the end of innocence, the darkness of man's heart, and the fall through the air of the true, wise friend called Piggy.
   > The officer, surrounded by these noises, was moved and a little embarrassed. He turned away from them to give them time to pull themselves together; and waited, allowing his eyes to rest on the trim cruiser in the distance.

2. *Anita and Me*

You are advised to spend about 45 minutes on this question.

You should use the extract below and your knowledge of the whole novel to answer this question.

Write about Meena's family's feelings about Tollington.

In your response you should:
- refer to the extract and the novel as a whole;
- show your understanding of characters and events in the novel. [40]

5 of this question's marks are allocated for accuracy in spelling, punctuation and the use of vocabulary and sentence structures.

Whenever my father got sick of our three-up-three-down with its high uneven walls and narrow winding stairs, sick of the damp in the pantry, the outside toilet, the three buses it took to get to work, taking a bath in our bike shed and having to whisper when he wanted to shout, he'd turn to my mother and say, 'You wanted this house, remember that.'

My mother grew up in a small Punjabi village not far from Chandigarh. As she chopped onions for the evening meal or scrubbed the shine back onto a steel pan or watched the clouds of curds form in a bowl of slowly setting homemade yoghurt, any action with a rhythm, she would begin a mantra about her ancestral home. She would chant of a three-storeyed flat-roofed house, blinkered with carved wooden shutters around a dust yard where an old-fashioned pump stood under a mango tree.

She would talk of running with her tin mug to the she-goat tethered to the tree and, holding the mug under its nipples, pulling down a foaming jet of milk straight into her father's morning tea. She spoke of the cobra who lived in the damp grasses beneath the fallen apples in the vast walled orchard, of the peacocks whose keening kept her awake on rainy monsoon nights, of her Muslim neighbours whom they always made a point of visiting in festivals, bringing sweetmeats to emphasise how the land they shared was more important than the religious differences that would soon tear the Punjab in two.

Yet, in England, when all my mother's friends made the transition from relatives' spare rooms and furnished lodgings to homes of their own, they all looked for something 'modern', 'It's really up-to-date, Daljit,' one of the Aunties would preen as she gave us the grand tour of her first proper home in England. 'Look at the extra strong flush system…Can opener on the wall…Two minutes walk to all local amenities…' But my mother knew what she wanted. When she stepped off the bus in Tollington, she did not see the outside lavvy or the apology for a garden or the medieval kitchen, she saw fields and trees, light and space, and a horizon that welcomed the sky which, on a warm night and through squinted eyes, could almost look something like home.

3. **Never Let Me Go**

You are advised to spend about 45 minutes on this question.

You should use the extract below and your knowledge of the whole novel to answer this question.

Write about how Ishiguro explores ideas about what it means to be human.

In your response you should:
- refer to the extract and the novel as a whole;
- show your understanding of characters and events in the novel. [40]

5 of this question's marks are allocated for accuracy in spelling, punctuation and the use of vocabulary and sentence structures.

Ruth gave him an irritated look. 'Tommy, please shut up with all this "bit of fun" stuff. No one's listening.' Then turning to Chrissie and Rodney she went on: 'I didn't want to say when you first told me about this. But look, it was never on. They don't ever, *ever*, use people like that woman. Think about it. Why would she want to? We all know it, so why don't we all face it. We're not modelled from that sort…'

'Ruth,' I cut in firmly. 'Ruth, don't.'

But she just carried on. 'We all know it. We're modelled from *trash*. Junkies, prostitutes, winos, tramps. Convicts, maybe, just so long as they aren't psychos. That's what we come from. We all know it, so why don't we say it? A woman like that? Come on. Yeah, right, Tommy. A bit of fun. Let's have a bit of fun pretending. That other woman in there, her friend, the old one in the gallery. *Art* students, that's what she thought we were. Do you think she'd have talked to us like that if she'd known what we really were? What do you think she'd have said if we'd asked her? "Excuse me, but do you think your friend was ever a clone model?" She'd have thrown us out. We know it, so we might as well just say it. If you want to look for possibilities, if you want to do it properly, then you look in the gutter. You look in rubbish bins. Look down the toilet, that's where you'll find where we all came from.'

4. **The Woman in Black**

You are advised to spend about 45 minutes on this question.

You should use the extract below and your knowledge of the whole novel to answer this question.

Write about how Hill uses places to create atmosphere in *The Woman in Black*.

In your response you should:
- refer to the extract and the novel as a whole;
- show your understanding of characters and events in the novel. [40]

5 of this question's marks are allocated for accuracy in spelling, punctuation and the use of vocabulary and sentence structures.

During the night the wind rose. As I had lain reading I had become aware of the stronger gusts that blew every so often against the casements. But when I awoke abruptly in the early hours it had increased greatly in force. The house felt like a ship at sea, battered by the gale that came roaring across the open marsh. Windows were rattling everywhere and there was the sound of moaning all down the chimneys of the house and whistling through every nook and cranny.

At first I was alarmed. Then, as I lay still, gathering my wits, I reflected on how long Eel Marsh House had stood here, steady as a lighthouse, quite alone and exposed, bearing the brunt of winter after winter of gales and driving rain and sleet and spray. It was unlikely to blow away tonight. And then, those memories of childhood began to be stirred again and I dwelt nostalgically upon all those nights when I had lain in the warm and snug safety of my bed in the nursery at the top of our family house in Sussex, hearing the wind rage round like a lion, howling at the doors and beating upon the windows but powerless to reach me. I lay back and slipped into that pleasant, trance-like state somewhere between sleeping and waking, recalling the past and all its emotions and impressions vividly, until I felt I was a small boy again.

Then from somewhere, out of that howling darkness, a cry came to my ears, catapulting me back into the present and banishing all tranquillity.

I listened hard. Nothing. The tumult of the wind, like a banshee, and the banging and rattling of the window in its old, ill-fitting frame. Then yes, again, a cry, that familiar cry of desperation and anguish, a cry for help from a child somewhere out on the marsh.

5. *Oranges are not the Only Fruit*

You are advised to spend about 45 minutes on this question.

You should use the extract below and your knowledge of the whole novel to answer this question.

Write about the part played by religion in Jeanette's life.

In your response you should:
- refer to the extract and the novel as a whole;
- show your understanding of characters and events in the novel. [40]

5 of this question's marks are allocated for accuracy in spelling, punctuation and the use of vocabulary and sentence structures.

Sunday was the Lord's day, the most vigorous day of the whole week; we had a radiogram at home with an imposing mahogany front and a fat Bakelite knob to twiddle for the stations. Usually we listened to the Light Programme, but on Sundays always the World Service, so that my mother could record the progress of our missionaries. Our Missionary Map was very fine. On the front were all the countries and on the back a number chart that told you about Tribes and their Peculiarities. My favourite was Number 16, *The Buzule of Carpathian*. They believed that if a mouse found your hair clippings and built a nest with them you got a headache. If the nest was big enough, you might go mad. As far as I knew no missionary had yet visited them.

My mother got up early on Sundays and allowed no one into the parlour until ten o'clock. It was her place of prayer and meditation. She always prayed standing up, because of her knees, just as Bonaparte always gave orders from his horse, because of his size. I do not think the relationship my mother enjoyed with God had a lot to do with positioning. She was Old Testament through and through. Not for her the meek and paschal Lamb, she was out there, up front with the prophets, and much given to sulking under trees when the appropriate destruction didn't materialise. Quite often it did, her will or the Lord's I can't say.

As soon as 'Vengeance is mine saith the Lord' boomed through the wall into the kitchen, I put the kettle on. The time it took to boil the water and brew the tea was just about the length of her final item, the sick list. She was very regular. I put the milk in, in she came, and taking a great gulp of tea said one of three things.

'The Lord is good' (steely-eyed into the back yard).

'What sort of tea is this?' (steely-eyed at me).

'Who was the oldest man in the Bible?'

6. *The Curious Incident of the Dog in the Night-Time*

You are advised to spend about 45 minutes on this question.

You should use the extract below and your knowledge of the whole play to answer this question.

Write about how Christopher changes as a result of the death of Wellington.

In your response you should:
- refer to the extract and the play as a whole;
- show your understanding of characters and events in the play. [40]

5 of this question's marks are allocated for accuracy in spelling, punctuation and the use of vocabulary and sentence structures.

CHRISTOPHER	I'm sorry.
ED	It's OK.
CHRISTOPHER	I didn't kill Wellington.
ED	I know.
	Christopher you have to stay out of trouble, OK?
CHRISTOPHER	I didn't know I was going to get into trouble. I like Wellington and I went to say hello to him, but I didn't know that someone had killed him.
ED	Just try and keep your nose out of other people's business.
CHRISTOPHER	I am going to find out who killed Wellington.
ED	Were you listening to what I was saying, Christopher?
CHRISTOPHER	Yes I was listening to what you were saying but when someone gets murdered you have to find out who did it so that they can be punished.
ED	It's a bloody dog Christopher, a bloody dog.
CHRISTOPHER	I think dogs are important too. I think some dogs are cleverer than some people. Steve, for example, who comes to school on Thursdays needs help eating his food and he probably couldn't even fetch a stick.
ED	I said leave it for God's sake.
CHRISTOPHER	Are you sad about Wellington?
ED	Yes Christopher you could say that. You could very well say that.

7. **A Taste of Honey**

You are advised to spend about 45 minutes on this question.

You should use the extract below and your knowledge of the whole play to answer this question.

Write about how Delaney presents different ideas about motherhood.

In your response you should:
- refer to the extract and the play as a whole;
- show your understanding of characters and events in the play. [40]

5 of this question's marks are allocated for accuracy in spelling, punctuation and the use of vocabulary and sentence structures.

GEOF	You can get rid of babies before they're born, you know.
JO	I know, but I think that's terrible.
GEOF	When's it due?
JO	Reckon it up from Christmas.
GEOF	About September.
JO	Yes.
GEOF	What are you going to do? You can't be on your own.
JO	There's plenty of time.
GEOF	Got any money?
JO	Only my wages and they don't last long. By the time I've bought all I need, stockings and make-up and things, I've got nothing left.
GEOF	You can do without make-up.
JO	I can't. I look like a ghost without it.
GEOF	At your age?
JO	What's age got to do with it? Anyway, I'm not working for much longer. I'm not having everybody staring at me.
GEOF	How are you going to manage then?
JO	There's no need for you to worry about it.
GEOF	Somebody's got to. Anyway, I like you.
JO	I like you too.
GEOF	Your mother should know.
JO	Why?
GEOF	Well, she's your mother. Do you know her address?

8. An Inspector Calls

You are advised to spend about 45 minutes on this question.

You should use the extract below and your knowledge of the whole play to answer this question.

Write about the role and significance of Inspector Goole and how he is presented in the play.

In your response you should:
- refer to the extract and the play as a whole;
- show your understanding of characters and events in the play. [40]

5 of this question's marks are allocated for accuracy in spelling, punctuation and the use of vocabulary and sentence structures.

INSPECTOR	You helped – but you didn't start it. [*Rather savagely, to* BIRLING] You started it! She wanted twenty-five shillings a week instead of twenty-two and sixpence. You made her pay a heavy price for that. And now she'll make you pay a heavier price still.
BIRLING	[*unhappily*] Look, Inspector – I'd give thousands – yes, thousands –
INSPECTOR	You're offering money at the wrong time, Mr Birling. [*He makes a move as if concluding the session, possibly shutting up notebook, etc. Then surveys them sardonically.*] No, I don't think any of you will forget. Nor that young man, Croft, though he at least had some affection for her and made her happy for a time. Well, Eva Smith's gone. You can't do her any more harm. And you can't do her any good now, either. You can't even say 'I'm sorry, Eva Smith.'
SHEILA	[*who is crying quietly*] That's the worst of it.
INSPECTOR	But just remember this. One Eva Smith has gone – but there are millions and millions of Eva Smiths and John Smiths still left with us, with their lives, their hopes and fears, their sufferings, and chance of happiness, all intertwined with our lives, with what we think and say and do. We don't live alone. We are members of one body. We are responsible for each other. And I tell you the time will soon come when, if men will not learn that lesson, then they will be taught it in fire and blood and anguish. Good night.

9. **The History Boys**

You are advised to spend about 45 minutes on this question.

You should use the extract below and your knowledge of the whole play to answer this question.

Write about how Bennett shows friendships between teachers and boys in the play.

In your response you should:
- refer to the extract and the play as a whole;
- show your understanding of characters and events in the play. [40]

5 of this question's marks are allocated for accuracy in spelling, punctuation and the use of vocabulary and sentence structures.

MRS LINTOTT	It's a test. A way of finding out if you've ceased to be a teacher and become a friend.
	He's a bright boy. You'll see. Next time he'll go further. What else did you talk about?
IRWIN	Nothing.
	No. Nothing.
	Mrs Lintott goes.
	Posner.
POSNER	Sir?
IRWIN	What goes on in Mr Hector's lessons?
POSNER	Nothing, sir.
	Anyway, you shouldn't ask me that, sir.
IRWIN	Quid pro quo.
POSNER	I have to go now, sir.
IRWIN	You learn poetry. Off your own bat?
POSNER	Sometimes.
	He makes you want to, sir.
IRWIN	How?
POSNER	It's a conspiracy, sir.
IRWIN	Who against?
POSNER	The world, sir. I hate this, sir. Can I go?
IRWIN	Is that why he locks the door?
POSNER	So that it's not part of the system, sir. Time out. Nobody's business. Useless knowledge.
	Can I go, sir?
IRWIN	Why didn't you ask Mr Hector about Dakin?
POSNER	I wanted advice, sir.

10. *Blood Brothers*

You are advised to spend about 45 minutes on this question.

You should use the extract below and your knowledge of the whole play to answer this question.

Write about the character of Linda, her relationships with Mickey and Edward, and how she is presented throughout the play.

In your response you should:
- refer to the extract and the play as a whole;
- show your understanding of characters and events in the play. [40]

5 of this question's marks are allocated for accuracy in spelling, punctuation, and the use of vocabulary and sentence structures.

LINDA	I hate them! LINDA *notices* MICKEY *quietly crying*. What's up?
MICKEY	I don't wanna die.
LINDA	But y'have to Mickey. Everyone does. (*She starts to dry his tears*) Like your twinny died, didn't he, when he was a baby. See, look on the bright side of it, Mickey. When you die you'll meet your twinny again, won't y'?
MICKEY	Yeh.
LINDA	An' listen Mickey, if y' dead, there's no school, is there?
MICKEY	(*smiling*) An' I don't care about our Sammy, anyway. Look. (*He produces an air pistol*.) He thinks no-one knows he's got it. But I know where he hides it.
LINDA	(*impressed*) Ooh…gis a go.
MICKEY	No…come on, let's go get Eddie first.
LINDA	Who?
MICKEY	Come on, I'll show y'. *They go as if to* EDWARD'S *garden*.
MICKEY	(*loud but conspiratorially*) Eddie…Eddie…y'comin' out?
EDWARD	I…My mum says I haven't got to play with you.
MICKEY	Well, my mum says I haven't got to play with you. But take no notice of mothers. They're soft. Come on, I've got Linda with me. She's a girl but she's all right.

SECTION B (19th Century Prose)

*Answer on **one** text only.*

11. ***A Christmas Carol***

You are advised to spend about 45 minutes on this question.

You should use the extract below and your knowledge of the whole novel to answer this question.

Write about how Scrooge has been shaped by his past experiences.

In your response you should:
- refer to the extract and the novel as a whole;
- show your understanding of characters and events in the novel;
- refer to the contexts of the novel. [40]

'Your reclamation, then. Take heed!'

It put out a strong hand as it spoke, and clasped him gently by the arm.

'Rise! And walk with me!'

It would have been in vain for Scrooge to plead that the weather and the hour were not adapted to pedestrian purposes; that bed was warm, and the thermometer a long way below freezing; that he was clad but lightly in his slippers, dressing-gown, and nightcap; and that he had a cold upon him at that time. The grasp, though gentle as a woman's hand, was not to be resisted. He rose: but, finding that the spirit made towards the window, clasped its robe in supplication.

'I am a mortal,' Scrooge remonstrated, 'and liable to fall.'

'Bear but a touch of my hand there,' said the Spirit, laying it upon his heart, 'and you shall be upheld in more than this!'

As the words were spoken, they passed through the wall, and stood upon an open country road, with fields on either hand. The city had entirely vanished. Not a vestige of it was to be seen. The darkness and the mist had vanished with it, for it was a clear, cold, winter day, with the snow upon the ground.

'Good Heaven!' said Scrooge, clasping his hands together as he looked about him. 'I was bred in this place. I was a boy here!'

The Spirit gazed upon him mildly. Its gentle touch, though it had been light and instantaneous, appeared still present to the old man's sense of feeling. He was conscious of a thousand odours floating in the air, each one connected with a thousand thoughts, and hopes, and joys, and cares long, long forgotten!

'Your lip is trembling,' said the Ghost. 'And what is that upon your cheek?' Scrooge muttered, with an unusual catching in his voice, that it was a pimple; and begged the ghost to lead him where he would.

12. ***Silas Marner***

You are advised to spend about 45 minutes on this question.

You should use the extract below and your knowledge of the whole novel to answer this question.

Write about how Eliot presents Godfrey Cass as a father and a husband.

In your response you should:
- refer to the extract and the novel as a whole;
- show your understanding of characters and events in the novel;
- refer to the contexts of the novel.

[40]

Nancy looked at Godfrey with a pained questioning glance. But his eyes were fixed on the floor, where he was moving the end of his stick, as if he were pondering on something absently. She thought there was a word which might perhaps come better from her lips than from his.

'What you say is natural, my dear child – it's natural you should cling to those who've brought you up,' she said mildly; 'but there's a duty you owe to your lawful father. There's perhaps something to be given up on more sides than one. When your father opens his home to you, I think it's right you shouldn't turn your back on it.'

'I can't feel as I've got any father but one,' said Eppie impetuously while the tears gathered. 'I've always thought of a little home where he'd sit i' the corner, and I should fend and do everything for him: I can't think o' no other home. I wasn't brought up to be a lady, and I can't turn my mind to it. I like the working folks, and their houses, and their ways. And,' she ended passionately, while the tears fell, 'I've promised to marry a working man as'll live with father, and help me to take care of him.'

Godfrey looked up at Nancy with a flushed face and a smarting dilation of the eyes. This frustration of a purpose towards which he had set out under the exalted consciousness that he was about to compensate in some degree for the greatest demerit of his life, made him feel the air of the room stifling.

'Let us go now,' he said, in an under-tone.

'We won't talk any longer now,' said Nancy, rising. 'We're your well-wishers, my dear – and yours too, Marner. We shall come and see you again. It's getting late.'

In this way she covered her husband's abrupt departure, for Godfrey had gone straight to the door, unable to say more.

13. ***Pride and Prejudice***

   You are advised to spend about 45 minutes on this question.

   You should use the extract below and your knowledge of the whole novel to answer this question.

   Write about Mr and Mrs Bennet and how they are presented throughout the novel.

   In your response you should:
   - refer to the extract and the novel as a whole;
   - show your understanding of characters and events in the novel;
   - refer to the contexts of the novel. [40]

   Mrs Bennet was in fact too much overpowered to say a great deal while Sir William remained; but no sooner had he left than her feelings found a rapid vent. In the first place, she persisted in disbelieving the whole of the matter; secondly, she was very sure that Mr Collins had been taken in; thirdly, she trusted that they would never be happy together; and fourthly, that the match might be broken off. Two inferences, however, were plainly deduced from the whole. One, that Elizabeth was the real cause of all the mischief; and the other, that she herself had been barbarously used by them all; and on these two points she principally dwelt during the rest of the day. Nothing could console and nothing appease her. Nor did that day wear out her resentment. A week elapsed before she could see Elizabeth without scolding her, a month passed away before she could speak to Sir William or Lady Lucas without being rude, and many months were gone before she could at all forgive their daughter.

   Mr Bennet's emotions were much more tranquil on the occasion, and such as he did experience he pronounced to be of a most agreeable sort; for it gratified him, he said, to discover that Charlotte Lucas, whom he had been used to think tolerably sensible, was as foolish as his wife, and more foolish than his daughter!

14. ***War of the Worlds***

   You are advised to spend about 45 minutes on this question.

   You should use the extract below and your knowledge of the whole novel to answer this question.

   Write about how Wells presents the experience of people fleeing the Martians.

   In your response you should:
   - refer to the extract and the novel as a whole;
   - show your understanding of characters and events in the novel;
   - refer to the contexts of the novel. [40]

   > So you understand the roaring wave of fear that swept through the greatest city in the world just as Monday was dawning – the stream of flight rising swiftly to a torrent, lashing in a foaming tumult around the railway stations, banked up into a horrible struggle about the shipping in the Thames, and hurrying by every available channel northward and eastward. By ten o'clock the police organisation, and by midday even the railway organisations, were losing coherency, losing shape and efficiency, guttering, softening, running at last in that swift liquefaction of the social body.
   >
   > All the railway lines north of the Thames and the South-Eastern people at Cannon Street had been warned by midnight on Sunday, and trains were being filled. People were fighting savagely for standing-room in the carriages even at two o-clock. By three, people were being trampled and crushed even in Bishopgate Street, a couple of hundred yards or more from Liverpool Street station; revolvers were fired, people stabbed, and the policemen who had been sent to direct the traffic, exhausted and infuriated, were breaking the heads of the people they were called out to protect.
   >
   > And as the day advanced and the engine drivers and stokers refused to return to London, the pressure of the flight drove the people in an ever-thickening multitude away from the stations and along the northward-running roads. By midday a Martian had been seen at Barnes, and a cloud of slowly sinking black vapour drove along the Thames and across the flats of Lambeth, cutting off all escape over the bridges in its sluggish advance. Another bank drove over Ealing, and surrounded a little island of survivors on Castle Hill, alive, but unable to escape.

15. **Jane Eyre**

You are advised to spend about 45 minutes on this question.

You should use the extract below and your knowledge of the whole novel to answer this question.

Write about how Jane's position as a governess and her awareness of social class are explored throughout the novel.

In your response you should:
- refer to the extract and the novel as a whole;
- show your understanding of characters and events in the novel;
- refer to the contexts of the novel. [40]

I waited till the last deep and full vibration had expired – till the tide of talk, checked an instant, had resumed its flow; I then quitted my sheltered corner and made my exit by the side-door, which was fortunately near. Hence a narrow passage led into the hall: in crossing it, I perceived my sandal was loose; I stopped to tie it, kneeling down for that purpose on the mat at the foot of the staircase. I heard the dining-room door unclose; a gentleman came out; rising hastily, I stood face to face with him: it was Mr Rochester.

'How do you do?' he asked.

'I am very well, sir.'

'Why did you not come and speak to me in the room?'

I thought I might have retorted the question on him who put it: but I would not take that freedom. I answered –

'I did not wish to disturb you, as you seemed engaged, sir.'

'What have you been doing during my absence?'

'Nothing in particular; teaching Adele as usual.'

'And getting a good deal paler than you were – as I saw at first sight. What is the matter?'

'Nothing at all, sir.'

'Did you take any cold that night you half-drowned me?'

'Not in the least.'

'Return to the drawing room: you are deserting too early.'

'I am tired, sir.'

He looked at me for a minute.

'And a little depressed,' he said. 'What about? Tell me.'

16. **The Strange Case of Dr Jekyll and Mr Hyde**

You are advised to spend about 45 minutes on this question.

You should use the extract below and your knowledge of the whole novel to answer this question.

Write about how sympathetically Jekyll is presented at different points in the novel.

In your response you should:
- refer to the extract and the novel as a whole;
- show your understanding of characters and events in the novel;
- refer to the contexts of the novel.

[40]

The court was very cool and a little damp, and full of premature twilight, although the sky, high up overhead, was still bright with sunset. The middle one of the three windows was half way open; and sitting close beside it, taking the air with an infinite sadness of mien, like some disconsolate prisoner, Utterson saw Dr Jekyll.

'What! Jekyll!' he cried. 'I trust you are better.'

'I am very low, Utterson,' replied the doctor drearily, 'very low. It will not last long, thank God.'

'You stay too much indoors,' said the lawyer. 'You should be out, whipping up the circulation like Mr Enfield and me. (This is my cousin Mr Enfield – Mr Enfield – Dr Jekyll.) Come now; get your hat and take a quick turn with us.'

'You are very good,' sighed the other. 'I should like to very much; but no, no, no, it is quite impossible; I dare not. But indeed, Utterson, I am very glad to see you; this is really a great pleasure; I would ask you and Mr Enfield up, but the place is really not fit.'

'Why then,' said the lawyer, good-naturedly, 'the best thing we can do is to stay down here and speak to you from where we are.'

'That is just what I was about to venture to propose,' returned the doctor with a smile. But the words were hardly uttered, before the smile was struck out of his face and succeeded by an expression of such abject terror and despair, as froze the very blood of the two gentlemen below. They saw it but for a glimpse, for the window was instantly thrust down; but that glimpse had been sufficient, and they turned and left the court without a word. In silence they traversed the by-street; and it was not until they had come into a neighbouring thoroughfare, where even upon a Sunday there were still some stirrings of life, that Mr Utterson at last turned and looked at his companion. They were both pale; and there was an answering horror in their eyes.

'God forgive us, God forgive us,' said Mr Utterson.

But Mr Enfield only nodded his head very seriously, and walked on once more in silence.

SECTION C Unseen Poetry

*Answer **both** part (a) **and** part (b).*

You are advised to spend about 20 minutes on part (a) and about 40 minutes on part (b).

17. Read the two poems, *Past and Present* by Thomas Hood and *The Swing* by Robert Louis Stevenson. In both of these poems the poets write about childhood.

(a) Write about the poem *Past and Present* by Thomas Hood, and its effect on you. [15]

You may wish to consider:
- what the poem is about and how it is organised;
- the ideas the poet may have wanted us to think about;
- the poet's choice of words, phrases and images and the effects they create;
- how you respond to the poem.

Past and Present

I remember, I remember
The house where I was born,
The little window where the sun
Came peeping in at morn;
He never came a wink too soon
Nor brought too long a day;
But now, I often wish the night
Had borne my breath away.

I remember, I remember
The roses, red and white,
The violets and the lily-cups –
Those flowers made of light!
The lilacs where the robin built,
And where my brother set
The laburnum on his birthday, –
The tree is living yet.

I remember, I remember
Where I was used to swing,
And thought the air must rush as fresh
To swallows on the wing;
My spirit flew in feathers then
That is so heavy now,
And summer pools could hardly cool
The fever on my brow.

I remember, I remember
The fir trees dark and high;
I used to think their slender tops
Were close against the sky:
It was a childish ignorance,
But now 'tis little joy
To know I'm farther off from Heaven
Than when I was a boy.

Thomas Hood

(b) Now compare *Past and Present* by Thomas Hood and *The Swing* by Robert Louis Stevenson. [25]

You should compare:
- what the poems are about and how they are organised;
- the ideas the poets may have wanted us to think about;
- the poets' choice of words, phrases and images and the effects they create;
- how you respond to the poems.

The Swing

How do you like to go up in a swing,
Up in the air so blue?
Oh I do think it the pleasant thing
Ever a child can do.

Up in the air and over the wall,
Till I can see so wide,
River and trees and cattle and all
Over the countryside –

Till I look down on the garden green,
Down on the roof so brown –
Up in the air I go flying again,
Up in the air and down!

Robert Louis Stevenson

For answers worth 5 or more marks, detailed mark schemes are given, which include the skills shown in your answer and examples of the content you might have included. **They are not full or model answers.** *Examples of suggested content should not be treated as 'checklists' and valid alternatives will be rewarded. Look at the mark scheme and decide which description is closest to your answer.*

Please note that the exam board does not decide on grade boundaries until after the marking process has been completed, so grade equivalents given here are approximate and should be treated with caution.

ENGLISH LANGUAGE

COMPONENT 1: 20th Century Literature Reading and Creative Prose Writing

Section A: 20th Century Literature Reading

Pages 4–6

A1. Any **five** from:
- he is visiting the doctor
- he is not well/he is ill
- he works in a bar
- he works in the Bowery (in a slum)
- he gets up at 5 o'clock in the morning
- he goes for long walks in Central Park
- he has been to Ireland before/he would like to return to Ireland
- he comes from Ireland/Ireland is his home.

[1 mark for each up to a maximum of 5]

A2. [Maximum 5 marks]

Marks	Skills
5 (Grades 8–9)	You have made accurate and perceptive comments about life in Duncannon and have provided detailed analysis of how the writer uses language to achieve effects and influence the reader. You have explored subtleties of the writer's techniques in relation to how the reader is influenced. You have used well-considered and accurate subject terminology to support your comments.
4 (Grades 6–7)	You have made accurate comments about life in Duncannon and have begun to analyse how the writer uses language to achieve effects and influence the reader. You have used relevant subject terminology to support your comments.
3 (Grades 4–5)	You have made some comments about life in Duncannon and have begun to show understanding of how the writer uses language to achieve effects and influence the reader. You might have used some relevant subject terminology to support your comments.
2 (Grades 2–3)	You have identified some straightforward aspects of life in Duncannon. You might have used some relevant subject terminology.
1 (U–Grade 1)	You have identified and begun to comment on some aspects of life in Duncannon.

Examples of details that you might have explored or commented on:
- Duncannon is where Bryden was born (native village)
- it is built on the rocks
- it is built on a headland in a lake
- it is rural and agricultural
- there is a Georgian mansion
- children from different social classes/backgrounds mix
- villagers worked for the people at the big house
- there is a sense of a community working together
- the villagers were hardworking
- we are given Bryden's view of the village, which is nostalgic
- life in Duncannon might have changed since Bryden last saw it.

A3. [Maximum 10 marks]

Marks	Skills
9–10 (Grades 8–9)	You have made accurate and perceptive comments about the journey and the description of Mike Scully. You have provided detailed analysis of how the writer uses language to achieve effects. You have explored subtleties of the writer's techniques. You have used well-considered and accurate subject terminology to support your comments effectively.
7–8 (Grades 6–7)	You have made accurate comments about the journey and the description of Mike Scully. You have begun to analyse how the writer uses language to achieve effects. You have used relevant subject terminology to support your comments effectively.

5–6 (Grades 4–5)	You have explained how the journey and Mike Scully are described. You have begun to show understanding of how the writer uses language to achieve effects. You might have used some relevant subject terminology to support your comments.
3–4 (Grades 2–3)	You have identified and given some straightforward comments about the journey and Mike Scully. You might have used some relevant subject terminology.
1–2 (U–Grade 1)	You have identified and begun to comment on some aspects of the journey and Mike Scully.

Examples of details that you might have explored or commented on:
- the station is unchanged (repetition of 'same')
- the village seems a long way from the station
- the distance did not bother Bryden when he was younger but he does not feel strong enough to walk now
- it is a pleasant evening/good weather ('the evening tempted him')
- Bryden passes the time talking to the boy who drives the car
- while the boy is curious about him, he uses the journey to find out about the village
- he is looking for both general gossip ('who was still living in the village') and practical information ('a clean lodging')
- the subject of Mike Scully is introduced through discussion about lodgings
- Mike would appear to be comparatively well-off (with a 'fine house with a concrete floor')
- there is a sense, conveyed comically, that Duncannon people's experience is limited and their expectations low as they can be impressed by a concrete floor
- Bryden and Mike have something in common as Mike has also 'been away'
- Mike has not achieved his ambition of being a jockey
- Mike's past shows the traditional nature of rural life and its hierarchy (he was 'in a situation at the Big House')
- Bryden's memory of Mike is vague
- the boy's account of Mike shows how things and people have changed in Bryden's absence
- all the information is given through reported (indirect) speech
- focus is entirely on the conversation that takes place on the journey, with no description of scenery, etc.

A4. [Maximum 10 marks]

Marks	Skills
9–10 (Grades 8–9)	You have made accurate and perceptive comments about how a wide range of examples show the differences between the men and their reactions to each other. You have provided detailed analysis of how the writer uses language and the organisation of events to achieve effects and influence the reader. You have explored subtleties of the writer's techniques. You have used well-considered and accurate subject terminology to support your comments effectively.
7–8 (Grades 6–7)	You have made accurate comments about how a range of different examples show the differences between the men and their reactions to each other. You have begun to analyse how the writer uses language and the organisation of events to achieve effects and influence the reader. You have used relevant subject terminology to support your comments effectively.
5–6 (Grades 4–5)	You have explained how a number of different examples show the differences between the men and their reactions to each other. You have begun to show understanding of how the writer uses language and the organisation of events to achieve effects and influence the reader. You might have used some relevant subject terminology to support your comments.
3–4 (Grades 2–3)	You have identified and given some straightforward comments on some examples of differences between the men and/or their reactions to each other. You might have used some relevant subject terminology.
1–2 (U–Grade 1)	You have identified and begun to comment on some examples of the differences between the men and/or their reactions to each other.

Examples of details that you might have explored or commented on:
- how the reader is given access to Bryden's thoughts about Mike
- Bryden's direct comparison of his experience to Mike's experience in going away and coming back
- the repetition of 'had come back'
- the difference between the distance they have travelled (King's County/America)
- Bryden's implied envy of Mike's house
- Bryden's thoughts described as a 'reverie' (a dream or fantasy), suggesting he sees Mike's life as better than his
- the sudden switch of focus from his thoughts about Mike to seeing him ('suddenly interrupted')
- the switch from reported speech with the boy to reported thoughts and then to direct speech
- description of Mike as a 'finely-built' man, suggesting he is healthier than Bryden
- Mike's shock at being addressed by Bryden ('astonished')
- emphasis on the distance between them, created by passing time ('he had forgotten Bryden even more completely…')
- 'many aunts and uncles' suggests the closeness of the village and connections between the men
- Mike's description of Bryden as 'fine' echoing 'finely-built'
- Bryden seen through Mike's eyes and described physically
- Mike's directness about Bryden's looks, 'thin' and 'sallow' reflecting his illness, in contrast with Mike's own health
- the warmth of Mike's traditional Irish greeting ('a thousand welcomes')
- how quickly Mike moves from shock and surprise, not recognising Bryden, to treating him as an old friend.

A5. [Maximum 10 marks]

Marks	Skills
9–10 (Grades 8–9)	You have given a persuasive evaluation of the text and its effects, supported by convincing, well-selected examples and purposeful textual references. You have shown engagement and involvement, taking an overview to make accurate and perceptive comments about the text as a whole. You have explored how the writer has created thoughts and feelings with insight.
7–8 (Grades 6–7)	You have given a critical evaluation of the text and its effects, supported by convincing, well-selected textual references. You have shown critical awareness and clear engagement with the text. You have explored how the writer has created thoughts and feelings.
5–6 (Grades 4–5)	You have given an evaluation of the text and its effects, supported by appropriate textual references. You have shown some critical awareness of the text as a whole and how the writer has created thoughts and feelings.
3–4 (Grades 2–3)	You have given a personal opinion, supported by straightforward textual references. You have shown limited engagement with the text as a whole and/or how the writer has created thoughts and feelings.
1–2 (U–Grade 1)	You have expressed a simple personal opinion with linked, basic textual reference.

Examples of details that you might have explored or commented on:
- readers first learn about Duncannon through Bryden's memories
- his memories are nostalgic and create a picture of an ideal rural community
- both this and his later description contrast with life in New York
- the writer uses the walk to Mike's house to show how the area has changed
- contrast between Bryden's memories of 'well forested' woods and the present reality ('wind-worn')
- triplet describing the woods focuses on decay and neglect
- Bryden asks about the practical consequences of this neglect for the villagers
- Mike's response suggests the (comparative) poverty of the landlord as well as his obstinacy, and how these affect the whole village
- this idea of the landlord's lack of care for the villagers contrasts with Bryden's earlier memories of playing with the children of 'the Big House'
- emphasis on 'his property' showing how property ownership gives power
- the village itself described as 'desolate'
- Bryden's remark that it is not 'as much lived in as it used to be' implies many villagers have left/emigrated
- the paradox of the sight of the chickens being 'strange and familiar' reflects both how his life has changed and how he is nostalgic for Ireland
- Mike's description of Bryden as 'one of ourselves' shows friendliness and warmth
- Mrs Scully is also welcoming but concerned about whether her accommodation is good enough for Bryden
- their living arrangements give an impression of rural poverty, despite the carman having described their house as the 'best house in the village'.

Section B: Creative Prose Writing

Page 7

[Maximum 40 marks]

When marking your work, look at the 'Communication and organisation' and 'Vocabulary, sentence structure, spelling and punctuation' columns separately. Decide which 'band' fits your answer and award a mark within that band according to whether you have met the statement **convincingly** (top of the band), **adequately** (middle) or **'just'** met it (bottom).

Marks	Communication and organisation	Vocabulary, sentence structure, spelling and punctuation
33–40 (Grades 8–9)	**20–24 marks** • your writing is fully coherent and controlled: plot and characterisation are developed with detail, originality and imagination • your writing is clearly and imaginatively organised: narrative is sophisticated and fully engages the reader's interest • you have used structural and grammatical features ambitiously to give your writing cohesion and coherence • you have communicated ambitiously and consistently conveyed precise meaning	**14–16 marks** • you have used appropriate and effective variation of sentence structures • virtually all your sentence construction is controlled and accurate • you have used a range of punctuation confidently and accurately • you have spelled almost all words, including complex irregular words, correctly • your control of tense and agreement is totally secure • you have used a wide range of ambitious vocabulary to create effect or convey precise meaning

25–32 (Grades 6–7)	**15–19 marks** • your writing is clearly controlled and coherent: plot and characterisation show convincing detail and some originality and imagination • your writing is clearly organised: narrative is purposefully shaped and developed • you have used structural and grammatical features accurately to support cohesion and coherence • you have communicated with some ambition and conveyed precise meaning	**11–13 marks** • you have used varied sentence structures to achieve effects • your sentence construction is secure • you have used a range of punctuation accurately • you have spelled almost all words, including irregular words, correctly • your control of tense and agreement is secure • you have used ambitious vocabulary with precision
16–24 (Grades 4–5)	**10–14 marks** • your writing is mostly controlled and coherent: plot and characterisation show some convincing detail and development • your writing is organised: narrative is purposefully shaped and developed • you have used structural and grammatical features with some accuracy to convey meaning • you have communicated clearly but with limited ambition	**7–10 marks** • you have used varied sentence structures • your sentence construction is mostly secure • you have used a range of punctuation, mostly accurately • you have spelled most words, including irregular words, correctly • your control of tense and agreement is mostly secure • your vocabulary is beginning to develop and is used with some precision
8–15 (Grades 2–3)	**5–9 marks** • your writing is sometimes controlled and coherent: plot and characterisation show some control • your writing is organised: narrative is beginning to have some shape and development • you have used structural and grammatical features to convey meaning • you have communicated clearly in a limited way	**4–6 marks** • you have used some varied sentence structures • your sentence construction shows some control • you have used a range of punctuation with some control • you have spelled most words correctly • your control of tense and agreement is generally secure • there is some range of vocabulary
1–7 (U–Grade 1)	**1–4 marks** • your writing shows basic control and coherence: there is a basic sense of plot and characterisation • your writing is organised in a basic way: paragraphs may be used for obvious divisions • you have sometimes used structural and grammatical features to convey meaning • your communication is limited but you have conveyed some meaning	**1–3 marks** • you have used a limited range of sentence structures • your sentence construction shows limited control • you have attempted to use punctuation • you have spelled some words correctly • your control of tense and agreement is limited • there is a limited range of vocabulary

(a) **There are many possible responses. Here is an example of *part* of a possible Grade 8–9 answer:**

Suddenly a massive edifice of stone appeared through the mist. A landscape that had seemed deserted as we rowed steadily, carefully across the loch – the only sound the regular splish-splash of our innocent oars – was now dominated by this ancient fortress: our home. It was beautiful but its beauty was cold and forbidding. How long had it stood sentinel over these dark waters? How long had it stood proudly among the rolling hills, a symbol of power? How long had it been a witness to the ebb and flow of human history?

(b) **There are many possible responses. Here is an example of *part* of a possible Grade 8–9 answer:**

When she saw the story on the six o'clock news she knew instantly. She wouldn't be able to say how she knew. When, days later, she told Stephen he called it a mother's instinct but she had never believed in such things: instinct, ESP, second sight. To sensible, rational mother-of-three Rhona Chapman such things belonged in fairy stories, not in the real world, the world in which she had brought up her children. How had this tragedy – this horror – this nightmare – managed to invade her world?

(c) **There are many possible responses. Here is an example of *part* of a possible Grade 8–9 answer:**

I sat on the park bench and thought about what the doctor had said. Good news. I should have been elated. I could have celebrated; leapt for joy; turned cartwheels; fallen to the ground and sobbed for joy. But I felt nothing. Well, not exactly nothing. I felt (and I don't know how to put this without potentially causing offence) disappointed. I knew this was not how I should have been feeling and I resisted it – at first. But it came like a great wave and knocked me off my feet. Then came another wave, a darker, more sinister wave. A new feeling overwhelmed me and I let myself drown in it. It was fear.

(d) **There are many possible responses. Here is an example of *part* of a possible Grade 8–9 answer:**

'I think you'd better sit down,' she said. 'I've got some news.'

The laughter stopped immediately. We all looked at her. Amy's face betrayed no emotion. Not a flicker of the eyelids. Not a quiver of the lip. She stood, straight-backed and steady, her face immobile as if carved in stone. Sphinx-like. I remembered Gran had once said something about still waters running deep. It made me impatient with Amy and her unnatural calmness.

'Okay, Amy. You've got our attention. Just say what you've got to say and go.'

'I was there,' she said. 'I saw everything you did. I told the police.' Then, still without any sign of emotion, she left the room. That was the last time I saw her.

COMPONENT 2: 19th and 21st Century Non-Fiction Reading and Transactional/Persuasive Writing

Section A: 19th and 21st Century Non-Fiction Reading

Pages 8–13

A1. [1 mark for each up to a maximum of 3]
- (a) London [1]
- (b) France [1]
- (c) Any **one** from: patience/skill/flair [1]

A2. [Maximum 10 marks]

Marks	Skills
9–10 (Grades 8–9)	You have made accurate and perceptive comments about a wide range of different examples from the text which might persuade readers to buy Archie Bold's products. You have provided detailed analysis of how the writer uses language and structure to achieve effects and influence the reader. You have used accurate subject terminology to support your comments effectively.
7–8 (Grades 6–7)	You have made accurate comments about a range of different examples from the text which might persuade readers to buy Archie Bold's products. You have begun to analyse how the writer uses language and structure to influence the reader. You have used subject terminology to support your comments effectively.
5–6 (Grades 4–5)	You have explained how different examples from the text might persuade readers to buy Archie Bold's products. You have begun to show how the writer uses language and structure to influence the reader. You have begun to use relevant subject terminology to support your comments.
3–4 (Grades 2–3)	You have identified and given straightforward comments about examples from the text which might persuade readers to buy Archie Bold's products.
1–2 (U–Grade 1)	You have identified and begun to comment on how Archie Bold is trying to persuade his readers, but you have struggled to engage with the text and/or the question.

Examples of details that you might have explored or commented on:
- use of the first person to connect to readers and emphasise the nature of the business
- use of a friendly and informal tone ('Hi')
- use of details about the writer's life and family
- the way he tells the story of his career
- the introduction of his wife and their romance
- his qualifications and experience
- use of technical terminology ('sous chef'; 'patissiere'; 'fermentation')
- mention of his local origins
- the 'Parisian sophistication' of the cakes appealing to snobbery
- 'traditional' British baking appealing to nostalgia
- emphasis on quality of ingredients and expertise of bakers
- use of fashionable terms like 'artisan'
- contrast with 'supermarket'/'industrial' products
- use of positive emotive vocabulary such as 'passion', 'love', 'heart' and 'soul'
- inclusion of details of many products to appeal to as many people as possible ('…wholemeal, crusty white, granary and even gluten-free')
- short paragraphs and simple sub-headings
- repetition of key words such as 'traditional', 'real' and 'local'
- inclusion of practical details such as opening hours and the website, making it easy for customers to buy
- final strapline linked to opening.

A3. [1 mark for each up to a maximum of 3]
- (a) chemist [1]
- (b) by kneading flour into dough in a short time (20 minutes) [1]
- (c) steam [1]

A4. [Maximum 10 marks]

Marks	Skills and examples of possible content
9–10 (Grades 8–9)	You have given a persuasive evaluation of the text and its effects, supported by convincing, well-selected examples and purposeful textual references. You have shown engagement and involvement, taking an overview to make perceptive comments on Dodd's views, e.g. 'By describing current bread-making processes in London and Paris in vivid and often quite disgusting terms, the writer convinces the reader of the need for change. In contrast, the description of the mill in Birmingham represents what he sees as the glorious future of bread-making, although to a modern reader it might seem impersonal and over-industrialised'.
7–8 (Grades 6–7)	You have given a critical evaluation of the text and its effects, supported by well-selected textual references. You have shown critical awareness and clear engagement with Dodd's views, e.g. 'I think that the writer effectively describes examples of good and bad practices in industrial bread-making and seems determined to improve things in London by following practice in Birmingham'.

5–6 (Grades 4–5)	You have given an evaluation of the text supported by appropriate textual references. You have shown some critical awareness of Dodd's views, e.g. 'I think that he gives convincing opinions that bread-making at the time was usually inefficient and gives examples of how it can be improved'.
3–4 (Grades 2–3)	You have given a personal opinion supported by straightforward textual references. You have shown some interaction with Dodd's views, e.g. 'I think he was right to be concerned about how bread was made because it was slow and could not produce enough'.
1–2 (U–Grade 1)	You have expressed a simple personal opinion with linked basic textual references but have struggled to engage with the text and/or the question, e.g. 'I think he wants more bread made because people are hungry'.

Examples of details that you might have explored or responded to in addition to the points given above:
- description of the roughness and unpleasant nature of bread-making in London
- sense of London bread-making being old fashioned
- emphasis on expertise and academic qualifications of the writers of the French report
- vivid account of the wasteful and unhealthy practices in Paris
- scientific and technological advances being made, e.g. by M. Rolland
- the strangeness of the lack of modern mills in London
- admiring description of the efficiency of the steam-powered mills in Birmingham
- emphasis on the quantity of loaves that are produced in these mills.

A5. [Maximum 4 marks]

Marks	Skills and examples of possible content
4 (Grades 7–9)	You have synthesised with clear understanding and provided an overview drawn from a range of relevant details from both texts, e.g. 'Lucy's mill was highly mechanised, producing ten times the amount of bread that Archie can make by hand. The ingredients of the bread have not changed much, though Archie produces a variety of different 'artisan' breads as well as cakes, whereas Lucy's bakery seems to have concentrated on standard loaves for working men. Archie's methods and practices might be seen as a reaction to the industrialisation of bread-making by firms like Lucy's in the nineteenth century'.
3 (Grades 5–6)	You have synthesised with some understanding a range of relevant details from both texts, e.g. 'Archie's is a 'village bakery' making about 200 loaves, in contrast to Lucy's huge bread mill, which made 2,000. Methods are different with Lucy's using steam power while Archie emphasises that his bread is all hand-made'.
2 (Grades 3–4)	You have selected a range of relevant material from both texts, e.g. 'Lucy's is one of six large bread mills in Birmingham and uses steam, whereas Archie does everything by hand and makes less bread'.
1 (Grades 1–2)	You have made some selection of relevant, but simple, detail from both texts, e.g. 'Archie's bakery is in Rotterthwaite but Lucy's is in Birmingham'.

A6. [Maximum 10 marks]

Marks	Skills and examples of possible content
9–10 (Grades 8–9)	You have made comparisons that are sustained and detailed, showing clear understanding of how they are conveyed, e.g. 'The writers have contrasting purposes. Dodd wants his readers to understand how bread-making methods could be improved. His piece is like an academic paper, explaining how bread is made and describing technological advances. Archie also explains bread-making, but he wants to drum up business for his own small bakery. Some of the terminology used is similar, e.g. 'mix/mixing', 'knead/kneading', and they describe the same basic ingredients, showing they both have expertise in the subject. However, they have opposing points of view on mechanisation. To Dodd, the traditional way of bread-making that he has observed is 'rude and primitive' and he makes it seem revolting and unhygienic. Therefore, steam mills must be an improvement. Archie, writing over 150 years later, claims to bake 'with the heart' and by using terms like 'real bread' implies there is something false and unhealthy about bread produced in factories'.
7–8 (Grades 6–7)	You have made detailed comparisons with valid comments on how they are conveyed, e.g. 'Both writers describe bread-making and have firm ideas about how this should be done, but their approaches are opposite. Archie Bold wants to return to making bread by hand. He paints a picture of everything being done properly in a nice family environment and is not interested in making huge amounts of bread. In contrast, Dodd sees bread-making by hand as inefficient and uses words like 'wriggling' and 'uncouthness' to make it sound unpleasant. To him, the big steam mills of Birmingham seem much better'.
5–6 (Grades 4–5)	You have identified similarities and differences and made some comparisons, commenting on how they are conveyed, e.g. 'Dodd describes how bread is made in Paris but does not think it should be made like this. He sees the use of machines as progress. Archie also describes bread-making but has the opposite attitude to machinery. He likes making small amounts of traditional bread by hand and thinks this is progressive'.
3–4 (Grades 2–3)	You have identified and given a straightforward description of some of the main similarities and differences, e.g. 'Dodd describes how bread is made but does not think it should be made like this. He thinks the way it is done in huge mills is better. Archie, however, likes making small amounts of bread by hand'.
1–2 (U–Grade 1)	You have identified basic similarities and/or differences, e.g. 'One of them thinks it is better to make bread with machines but the other does not like machines'.

Section B: Transactional/Persuasive Writing

Page 14

B1 & B2 [Maximum 20 marks for each question]

When marking your work, look at the 'Communication and organisation' and 'Vocabulary, sentence structure, spelling and punctuation' columns separately. Decide which 'band' fits your answer and award a mark within that band according to whether you have met the statement **convincingly** (top of the band), **adequately** (middle) or **'just'** met it (bottom).

Marks	Communication and organisation	Vocabulary, sentence structure, spelling and punctuation
18–20 (Grades 8–9)	**11–12 marks** • your writing shows sophisticated understanding of the purpose and format of the task • your writing shows sustained awareness of the reader/intended audience • you have used an appropriate register, confidently adapted to your purpose/audience • your content is ambitious, pertinent and sophisticated • your ideas are convincingly developed and supported by a range of details	**8 marks** • you have used appropriate and effective variation of sentence structures • virtually all your sentence construction is controlled and accurate • you have used a range of punctuation confidently and accurately • you have spelled almost all words, including complex irregular words, correctly • your control of tense and agreement is totally secure • you have used a wide range of ambitious vocabulary to create effect or convey precise meaning
13–17 (Grades 6–7)	**8–10 marks** • your writing shows consistent understanding of the purpose and format of the task • your writing shows secure awareness of the reader/intended audience • you have used an appropriate register, consistently adapted to your purpose/audience • your content is well-judged and detailed • your ideas are organised and coherently developed, supported by relevant details	**6–7 marks** • you have used varied sentence structures to achieve effects • your sentence construction is secure • you have used a range of punctuation accurately • you have spelled almost all words, including irregular words, correctly • your control of tense and agreement is secure • you have used ambitious vocabulary with precision
8–12 (Grades 4–5)	**5–7 marks** • your writing shows clear understanding of the purpose and format of the task • your writing shows clear awareness of the reader/intended audience • you have used an appropriate register, adapted for purpose/audience • your content is clear and appropriate • your ideas are clearly organised and supported by relevant details	**4–5 marks** • you have used varied sentence structures • your sentence construction is mostly secure • you have used a range of punctuation mostly accurately • you have spelled most words, including irregular words, correctly • your control of tense and agreement is mostly secure • your vocabulary is beginning to develop and is used with some precision
4–7 (Grades 2–3)	**3–4 marks** • your writing shows some awareness of the purpose and format of the task • your writing shows some awareness of the reader/intended audience • you have sometimes used an appropriate register, adapted to purpose/audience • your content is appropriate with some detail • your ideas are organised to some extent, supported by some details	**2–3 marks** • you have used some varied sentence structures • your sentence construction shows some control • you have used a range of punctuation with some control • you have spelled most words correctly • your control of tense and agreement is generally secure • there is some range of vocabulary
1–3 (U–Grade 1)	**1–2 marks** • your writing shows basic understanding of the purpose and format of the task • your writing shows occasional awareness of the reader/intended audience • you have sometimes attempted to use an appropriate register • your content is occasionally appropriate • you have made some basic attempt to organise your ideas	**1 mark** • you have used a limited range of sentence structure • your sentence construction shows limited control • you have attempted to use punctuation • you have spelled some words correctly • your control of tense and agreement is limited • there is a limited range of vocabulary

B1. There are many possible responses. Here is an example of *part* of a possible Grade 8–9 answer:

Councillor Roberts claims that banning 'junk' food from schools is no different from banning knives or guns. I would argue that it is completely different. Leaving to one side her unnecessary (and possibly inflammatory) use of emotive language, it is clear that there is a huge difference between carrying weapons and carrying certain foods. A pupil who enters a school building carrying a weapon can reasonably be assumed to have the intention of causing injury to others. A pupil who brings in a lunch box containing a packet of

Doritos and a Twix cannot – unless, of course, he or she intends to hit someone over the head with said lunch box. Yes, sweets and crisps can be harmful but only to the person who consumes them and only if that person consumes large quantities of them and does not have a balanced diet.

B2. There are many possible responses. Here is an example of *part* of a possible Grade 8–9 answer:

Most of all, our restaurant, 'The Place', fulfils a real need. Look at the High Street and you will see quite a few catering outlets; I counted nine on Saturday. Seven of these are part of well-known, mostly American-owned chains, of which three are coffee shops, two specialise in burgers, one in fried chicken and one in noodles. Of the two 'independents' one is the long-established Chung's Chippy and the other a vegan health food restaurant. Not one of them offers what 'The Place' will offer: a varied menu of good quality, locally produced, well-cooked food. Our High Street needs 'The Place'.

ENGLISH LITERATURE

COMPONENT 1: Shakespeare and Poetry

Section A: Shakespeare

Pages 16–27

Questions 1–6

Mark parts **(a)** and **(b)** separately, using the table below for guidance. Note that part **(a)** is marked out of **15** and part **(b)** out of **20**. Then look at the table for AO4 (spelling, punctuation and the use of vocabulary and sentence structures) to award additional marks out of **5** for part **(b)**. See below these tables for suggested content that you might have included or discussed for each question.

Marks	Skills
(a) 13–15 **(b) 16–20** **(Grades 8–9)**	• You have sustained focus on the task, including overview, conveying ideas with consistent coherence in an appropriate register. • You have taken a sensitive and evaluative approach to the task and analysed the text critically. • You have shown a perceptive understanding of the text, engaging fully, perhaps with some originality in your personal response. • Your response includes pertinent direct references to the text, including quotations. • You have analysed and appreciated the writer's use of language, form and structure. • You have made assured reference to meaning and effects, exploring and evaluating the way meaning and ideas are conveyed through language, structure and form. • You have used precise subject terminology in an appropriate context.
(a) 10–12 **(b) 13–16** **(Grades 6–7)**	• You have sustained focus on the task, conveying ideas with consistent coherence in an appropriate register. • You have taken a thoughtful approach to the task. • You have shown a secure understanding of key aspects of the text, with considerable engagement. • Your response includes well-chosen direct references to the text, including quotations. • You have discussed and increasingly analysed the writer's use of language, form and structure. • You have made thoughtful reference to the meaning and effects of stylistic features used by the writer. • You have used apt subject terminology.
(a) 7–9 **(b) 9–12** **(Grades 4–5)**	• You have focused on the task, conveying ideas with general coherence usually in an appropriate register. • You have taken a straightforward approach to the task. • You have shown understanding of key aspects of the text, with engagement. • Your response includes appropriate direct references to the text, including quotations. • You have commented on and begun to analyse the writer's use of language, form and structure. • You have made some reference to meaning and effects. • You have used relevant subject terminology.
(a) 4–6 **(b) 5–8** **(Grades 2–3)**	• You have shown some focus on the task, conveying ideas with some coherence, sometimes in an appropriate register. • You have taken a limited approach to the task. • You have shown some understanding of key aspects of the text, with some engagement. • Your response includes some direct references to the text, including some quotations. • You have recognised and made simple comments on the writer's use of language, form and structure. • You may have made limited reference to meaning and effects. • You may have used some relevant subject terminology.
(a) 1–3 **(b) 1–4** **(U–Grade 1)**	• You have shown limited focus on the task, conveying ideas with occasional coherence, sometimes in an appropriate register. • You have taken a simple approach to the task. • You have shown a basic understanding of some key aspects of the text, with a little engagement. • Your response includes some general reference to the text, perhaps including some quotations. • You have made generalised comments on the writer's use of language, form and structure. • You may have made basic reference to meaning and effects. • You may have used some subject terminology but not always accurately.

Questions **1–6** (part **(b)**): marks for AO4 (spelling, punctuation and the use of vocabulary and sentence structure):

Marks	Skills
4–5 (Grades 7–9)	• You have spelled and punctuated with consistent accuracy. • You have consistently used a wide range of vocabulary and sentence structures with accuracy. • You have achieved effective control of meaning.
2–3 (Grades 4–6)	• You have spelled and punctuated with considerable accuracy. • You have used a considerable range of vocabulary and sentence structures. • You have achieved general control of meaning.
1 (Grades 1–3)	• You have spelled and punctuated with reasonable accuracy. • You have used a reasonable range of vocabulary and sentence structures. • Any errors do not hinder meaning.

1. ***Romeo and Juliet***

   (a) **Your response might have included some of the following points:**
   - Friar Laurence's role as Romeo's confessor
   - his initial shock at hearing of Romeo's love for Juliet
   - his characterisation of Romeo and all young men as fickle
   - his reference to Romeo's love for Rosaline making him miserable
   - the idea that Romeo's love for Rosaline was learned by 'rote' and therefore not real
   - Romeo's claim that his love for Juliet is returned equally
   - Romeo's reference to the Friar's previous advice
   - the Friar's willingness to help Romeo and his idea that their love could end the feud
   - the Friar's use of exclamations and rhetorical questions
   - the respectful tone of Romeo towards the Friar.

   (b) **Your response might have included some of the following points:**
   - our knowledge (from the Prologue) that the lovers will die
   - the idea that their love is doomed because of the families' feud
   - Romeo's love for Juliet leading directly to the deaths of Tybalt and Mercutio
   - premonitions of death during the balcony scene
   - the imagery used during that scene
   - Juliet's reflections on death when she takes the poison
   - the horrific imagery she uses in that scene
   - the theatrical impact of waking in the tomb
   - the idea that the intensity of their love makes death inevitable
   - death and love together reconciling the families.

2. ***Macbeth***

   (a) **Your response might have included some of the following points:**
   - Macduff's use of a series of short questions to convey his shock and disbelief
   - the way his speech is broken up by caesuras
   - his acceptance of Malcolm's advice tempered by his assertion that he 'must also feel it as a man' and what that means
   - the way the scene gives Macduff personal motivation for revenge
   - sympathy from the audience for him as a husband and father
   - the impact of showing his emotions
   - his use of a metaphor comparing his children to vulnerable chickens and Macbeth to a bird of prey
   - use of religious references ('Heaven'; 'sinful')
   - his sense of his own responsibility ('not for their own demerits but for mine')
   - the strength and determination of his last speech.

   (b) **Your response might have included some of the following points:**
   - the witches' prophecy making him think about becoming king
   - his initial reaction to the prophecy showing his conscience
   - Lady Macbeth's influence in persuading him to murder Duncan
   - the murder of Banquo and attempted murder of Fleance showing his increasing paranoia and ruthlessness
   - the suffering of Scotland under his reign
   - the description of strange omens
   - the murders of Lady Macduff and her children showing a new level of cruelty
   - his continuing awareness of his own evil and his choice to embrace it
   - the role of the supernatural, e.g. the visions summoned by the witches
   - religious language and religious references
   - recurring motifs of sleep and blood.

3. ***Othello***

   (a) **Your response might have included some of the following points:**
   - how Iago takes the audience into his confidence
   - how this recalls the devils of medieval drama
   - sympathy from the audience for Othello as Iago admits his 'constant, loving, noble nature'
   - his claim to be motivated by Othello's adultery with Emilia
   - questions about whether he believes this and whether it could be true
   - teasing of the audience about what he will do next
   - how he raises the possibility that he is jealous, as well as envious, of Othello
   - his use of the imagery of poison
   - the ambiguity of his attitude to Othello shown in his language.

   (b) **Your response might have included some of the following points:**
   - Othello and Desdemona's marriage has defied convention
   - ideas about fathers' power over daughters and social conventions
   - Othello's marriage is based on love but there is a lack of understanding and trust
   - Emilia's marriage is also lacking in trust and honesty
   - both husbands are quick to accuse their wives of unfaithfulness
   - Desdemona is faithful, obedient and loving, as a wife would be expected to be
   - how the power is all with Othello and he exercises it in the most extreme way
   - Emilia is cynical about marriage ('it is their husbands' faults/if wives do fall')
   - the structural effect of the play starting with a marriage – the opposite of a happy ending
   - the use of crude language and animal imagery to describe sexual acts.

4. ***Much Ado about Nothing***

   (a) **Your response might have included some of the following points:**
   - his situation as a bastard, an outsider with no power
   - his claim to be honest and unwilling to pretend in order to gain favour

- the fact that this is his first appearance in the play
- the conversation being with his confidant, Conrad, suggesting that we can take what he says as the truth
- Conrad's advice to cooperate with Don Pedro, which he does not follow
- both characters' use of natural imagery
- the contrast between Conrad's 'harvest' and Don John's 'canker in a hedge'
- Don John's characterisation of himself as a muzzled dog and a caged bird
- how his bitterness and discontent seen here lay the foundation for his plotting.

(b) **Your response might have included some of the following points:**
- Hero's use of trickery to make Beatrice reveal her feelings
- how disguise is used in the masque to give characters freedom to tell the truth
- how Don John uses disguise maliciously to deceive
- how Don John's deception works and almost causes tragedy
- how deception is then used to trick Claudio into thinking Hero is dead to make him realise he loves her
- elements of magic in the final trick
- religious symbolism in Hero's 'return from the dead'
- the audience's awareness of the tricks and subsequent dramatic irony
- contrast between the playful trickery in the Beatrice/Benedick plot and the serious deceit and trickery in the Hero/Claudio plot.

5. *Henry V*

(a) **Your response might have included some of the following points:**
- awareness of the reality of theatre (the 'wooden O') and the need for the audience to use imagination
- how the speech paints a vivid picture of war using violent diction
- use of rhetorical questions and imperatives
- the assumption of (false?) modesty about the performance that is to come
- language used to downplay the experience of theatre ('unworthy scaffold'; 'cock-pit')
- references to classical mythology ('Mars'; 'Muse')
- the build-up of excitement and anticipation
- the way the speech assumes some prior knowledge of 'warlike Harry' and his achievements
- the idea that the play is to be a celebration of those achievements.

(b) **Your response might have included some of the following points:**
- the impact of the scene after Agincourt where the dead are collected
- references to the amount of blood shed, conveying the horror of the scene
- some sympathy for the French perhaps mixed with joy at the English triumph
- Henry's frequent references to God, claiming divine support for his war
- the political effects of war, victory establishing Henry's authority and reputation
- how this becomes a part of national identity
- the portrayal of looting and profiteering showing the less glorious aspects of war
- the range of characters involved, from different social classes and different parts of the country.

6. *The Merchant of Venice*

(a) **Your response might have included some of the following points:**
- Portia is in control, telling Bassanio what she wants
- she, however, is controlled by her father's will
- her obedience to her father's wishes
- her desire not to be 'forsworn'
- the importance of making a good marriage
- her desire to marry the man she loves
- her openness about her love for Bassanio, although saying that 'a maiden hath no tongue but thought', meaning she has no real power
- use of caesura, breaking up the speech
- use of modal verbs, such as 'may', 'would' and 'could'
- mixture of religious and classical references ('sin'; 'Fortune'; 'hell').

(b) **Your response might have included some of the following points:**
- probable lack of sympathy when he locks up his daughter
- how the audience might see him as a kill-joy and tyrant
- the effect of his anti-Christian sentiments
- his treatment of Lancelot making him unsympathetic
- consideration of the likely difference between Elizabethan and modern attitudes
- possible anti-Semitic feeling in some audiences
- how modern audiences are more likely to side with the underdog/minority character
- shift in sympathy from Jessica (when she elopes) to Shylock (when he hears about what she has done)
- possible lack of sympathy when he demands his 'pound of flesh'
- shift in sympathies during court scene as he is defeated and humiliated.

Section B: Poetry

Page 28

7. Mark parts **(a)** and **(b)** separately, using the table below. Mark part **(a)** first out of **15** and then part **(b)** out of **25**.

See below this table for suggested content that you might have included or discussed for each question.

Marks	Skills
(a) 13–15 (b) 21–25 (Grades 8–9)	• You have sustained focus on the task, including overview, conveying ideas with consistent coherence in an appropriate register. • You have taken a sensitive and evaluative approach to the task and analysed the text critically. • You have shown a perceptive understanding of the text, engaging fully, perhaps with some originality in your personal response. • Your response includes pertinent direct references to the text, including quotations. • You have analysed and appreciated the writers' use of language, form and structure. • You have made assured reference to meaning and effects, exploring and evaluating the way meaning and ideas are conveyed through language, structure and form.

		• You have used precise subject terminology in an appropriate context.
• You have shown an assured understanding of the relationship between texts and the contexts in which they were written, including (where relevant) those of period, location, social structures and literary contexts such as genre.
• You have shown assured understanding of contexts in which texts are engaged with by different audiences.
	(a) 10–12
(b) 16–20
(Grades 6–7)	• You have sustained focus on the task, conveying ideas with consistent coherence in an appropriate register.
• You have taken a thoughtful approach to the task.
• You have shown a secure understanding of key aspects of the text, with considerable engagement.
• Your response includes well-chosen direct references to the text, including quotations.
• You have discussed and increasingly analysed the writers' use of language, form and structure.
• You have made thoughtful reference to the meaning and effects of stylistic features used by the writer.
• You have used apt subject terminology.
• You have shown secure understanding of the relationship between texts and the contexts in which they were written, including (where relevant) those of period, location, social structures and literary contexts such as genre.
• You have shown secure understanding of contexts in which texts are engaged with by different audiences.
	(a) 7–9
(b) 11–15
(Grades 4–5)	• You have focused on the task, conveying ideas with general coherence usually in an appropriate register.
• You have taken a straightforward approach to the task.
• You have shown understanding of key aspects of the text, with engagement.
• Your response includes appropriate direct references to the text, including quotations.
• You have commented on and begun to analyse the writers' use of language, form and structure.
• You have made some reference to meaning and effects.
• You have used relevant subject terminology.
• You have shown understanding of the relationship between texts and the contexts in which they were written, including (where relevant) those of period, location, social structures and literary contexts such as genre.
• You have shown understanding of contexts in which texts are engaged with by different audiences.
	(a) 4–6
(b) 6–10
(Grades 2–3)	• You have shown some focus on the task, conveying ideas with some coherence, sometimes in an appropriate register.
• You have taken a limited approach to the task.
• You have shown some understanding of key aspects of the text, with some engagement.
• Your response includes some direct references to the text, including some quotations.
• You have recognised and made simple comments on the writers' use of language, form and structure.
• You may have made limited reference to meaning and effects.
• You may have used some relevant subject terminology.
• You have shown some understanding of the relationship between texts and the contexts in which they were written, including (where relevant) those of period, location, social structures and literary contexts such as genre.
• You have shown some understanding of contexts in which texts are engaged with by different audiences.
	(a) 1–3
(b) 1–5
(U–Grade 1)	• You have shown limited focus on the task, conveying ideas with occasional coherence, sometimes in an appropriate register.
• You have taken a simple approach to the task.
• You have shown a basic understanding of some key aspects of the text, with a little engagement.
• Your response includes some general reference to the text, perhaps including some quotations.
• You have remade generalised comments on the writers' use of language, form and structure.
• You may have made basic reference to meaning and effects.
• You may have used some subject terminology but not always accurately.
• You have shown limited understanding of the relationship between texts and the contexts in which they were written, including (where relevant) those of period, location, social structures and literary contexts such as genre.
• You have shown limited understanding of contexts in which texts are engaged with by different audiences.

7. **(a) Your response might have included some of the following points:**
   - the poet addresses the loved one directly
   - the opening question leads to a series of answers
   - repetition of 'I love thee' (anaphora)
   - compares love for the subject to her love and grief for family
   - compares love to religious faith
   - love seen as eternal, lasting beyond death
   - use of Petrarchan (Italian) sonnet, a traditional form for love poetry
   - use of caesura (broken lines) to convey her excitement and spontaneity, in contrast with the regularity of the form
   - the poem's context as one of a series of sonnets written to the poet's husband.

   (b) In your response you might have compared the poem to the following poems and made some of the following points:
   - 'The Manhunt' – also a woman addressing a man, but a persona rather than the poet, contrasting contemporary situation, less formal and regular, imagery of war
   - 'Valentine' – also expressing love through imagery but through a single extended metaphor rather than a series of different images, contrast in form, contrasting comic tone
   - 'Cozy Apologia' – calmness of settled love rather than the discovery of new love, contemporary tone, images of everyday life.

COMPONENT 2: Post-1914 Prose/Drama and Unseen Poetry

Section A: Post-1914 Prose/Drama

Pages 30–39

Questions 1–10 [maximum 40 marks]

Use the table below to mark your response out of **35**. Then look at the table for AO4 (spelling, punctuation and the use of vocabulary and sentence structures) to award additional marks out of **5**. See below these tables for suggested content that you might have included or discussed for each question.

Marks	Skills
29–35 (Grade 8–9)	• You have sustained focus on the task, including overview, conveying ideas with consistent coherence in an appropriate register. • You have taken a sensitive and evaluative approach to the task and analysed the text critically. • You have shown a perceptive understanding of the text, engaging fully, perhaps with some originality in your personal response. • Your response includes pertinent direct references to the text, including quotations. • You have analysed and appreciated the writer's use of language, form and structure. • You have made assured reference to meaning and effects, exploring and evaluating the way meaning and ideas are conveyed through language, structure and form. • You have used precise subject terminology in an appropriate context.
22–28 (Grades 6–7)	• You have sustained focus on the task, conveying ideas with consistent coherence in an appropriate register. • You have taken a thoughtful approach to the task. • You have shown a secure understanding of key aspects of the text, with considerable engagement. • Your response includes well-chosen direct references to the text, including quotations. • You have discussed and increasingly analysed the writer's use of language, form and structure. • You have made thoughtful reference to the meaning and effects of stylistic features used by the writer. • You have used apt subject terminology.
15–21 (Grades 4–5)	• You have focused on the task, conveying ideas with general coherence usually in an appropriate register. • You have taken a straightforward approach to the task. • You have shown understanding of key aspects of the text, with engagement. • Your response includes appropriate direct references to the text, including quotations. • You have commented on and begun to analyse the writer's use of language, form and structure. • You have made some reference to meaning and effects. • You have used relevant subject terminology.
8–14 (Grades 2–3)	• You have shown some focus on the task, conveying ideas with some coherence, sometimes in an appropriate register. • You have taken a limited approach to the task. • You have shown some understanding of key aspects of the text, with some engagement. • Your response includes some direct references to the text, including some quotations. • You have recognised and made simple comments on the writer's use of language, form and structure. • You may have made limited reference to meaning and effects. • You may have used some relevant subject terminology.
1–7 (U–Grade 1)	• You have shown limited focus on the task, conveying ideas with occasional coherence, sometimes in an appropriate register. • You have taken a simple approach to the task. • You have shown a basic understanding of some key aspects of the text, with a little engagement. • Your response includes some general reference to the text, perhaps including some quotations. • You have made generalised comments on the writer's use of language, form and structure. • You may have made basic reference to meaning and effects. • You may have used some subject terminology but not always accurately.

Questions **1–10**: marks for AO4 (spelling, punctuation and the use of vocabulary and sentence structure):

Marks	Skills
4–5 (Grades 7–9)	• You have spelled and punctuated with consistent accuracy. • You have consistently used a wide range of vocabulary and sentence structures. • You have achieved effective control of meaning.
2–3 (Grades 4–6)	• You have spelled and punctuated with considerable accuracy. • You have used a considerable range of vocabulary and sentence structures. • You have achieved general control of meaning.
1 (Grades 1–3)	• You have spelled and punctuated with reasonable accuracy. • You have used a reasonable range of vocabulary and sentence structure. • Any errors do not hinder meaning.

1. ***Lord of the Flies***

   Your response might have included some of the following points:
   - being British used as shorthand for being civilised
   - the boys' ideas of correct behaviour are entwined with being British
   - these ideas have been learned at home and at public school
   - the officer talks about British boys putting on a 'better show'
   - being British means coping with adversity
   - at the time the novel was written, Britain's role in the world was changing, with the Empire coming to an end
   - the concept of 'Britishness' alluded to by the officer is a male upper-class one
   - the influence on the novel of boys' adventure stories popular in the 19th and 20th centuries (including *Coral Island*) in which boys overcame danger
   - Britain was associated with colonialism and the events of the novel undermine the idea of colonialism
   - Golding's implicit criticism of all nation states, not just Britain, and their involvement in wars.

2. ***Anita and Me***

   Your response might have included some of the following points:
   - the house is old-fashioned and uncomfortable
   - Meena's father is 'sick of' it and the distance from his work
   - Tollington's situation in the countryside appeals to Meena's mother
   - she likes it because it reminds her of her home in the Punjab
   - she is seen as unusual or odd by other Indians, who want modern houses nearer the city
   - Tollington is a poor, run-down village
   - its size and sense of community appeal to the young Meena
   - the family is conscious of being the only Indian family and, therefore, the object of curiosity and prejudice
   - they are middle-class and better educated than most of the neighbours and sometimes look down on them
   - as Meena gets older she becomes more aware of racism and the differences between her and other Tollington people.

3. ***Never Let Me Go***

   Your response might have included some of the following points:
   - in the extract Ruth voices her feelings about being a clone, which no-one else has articulated
   - the word 'clone' is rarely used and for a long time readers might not realise the characters are clones
   - Ruth thinks the others are living a fantasy, trying to make themselves feel better
   - she associates clones with 'trash' – even worse than the worst humans
   - Kathy has hinted at these origins before and they may be right
   - in spite of clones knowing that they are different, they have human emotions and relationships
   - Kathy feels that their 'human' behaviour is learned, her friends imitating behaviour and relationships that they see on television
   - at the end, her feelings are no different from the feelings of any human
   - we see everything through a clone's eyes, leading us to wonder what the difference is between clones and humans
   - readers might ask whether it is/will be possible to create clones in this way and, if so, will they feel and think like humans?

4. ***The Woman in Black***

   Your response might have included some of the following points:
   - Eel House is isolated and cut off, giving a sense of loneliness and vulnerability
   - imagery such as the simile 'like a ship at sea' conveys a sense of danger
   - descriptions of the weather add to this sense
   - the weather is actually dangerous, but is also used to reflect the narrator's feelings (pathetic fallacy)
   - in the passage Kipps rationalises and momentarily banishes his fear
   - memories of a different, happier place create a sense of calm, lowering tension before it is heightened again
   - Eel House is a conventional setting for a ghost story in the Gothic tradition
   - the real tragedy, however, occurs in a pleasant, apparently safe place.

5. ***Oranges are not the Only Fruit***

   Your response might have included some of the following points:
   - her mother is committed to an evangelical, Old Testament form of Christianity
   - their church is central to their lives and forms a community different from the rest of the town
   - her mother is eccentric in her religious practice as in everything else
   - religion is written about with humour and Jeanette looks back affectionately on it
   - Bible stories and things like the missionary map appeal to the creative child
   - preaching and the Bible are of great importance to Jeanette – but is it faith or a love of literature and 'showing off'?
   - Jeanette's sexuality is not accepted by the church and she cannot stay in the church
   - religion seen as being oppressive and cruel.

6. ***The Curious Incident of the Dog in the Night-Time***

   Your response might have included some of the following points:
   - Christopher is concerned that he has been accused of killing Wellington
   - he likes facts and is not willing to let this go – he needs to know the truth
   - he applies his own logic to the case, based on dogs being as important as people
   - Ed's reaction suggests to the audience (but not to literal-minded Christopher) that he is hiding something
   - his investigation leads him to discover the truth about other things, e.g. his parents' marriage
   - he becomes more independent, taking the initiative and facing his fears (e.g. on the train)
   - other characters may begin to value him more – does he value them more?
   - he attributes his increased confidence and success to the incident ('I can because I went to London on my own.')
   - the audience is left wondering how much he can achieve ('Does that mean I can do anything?')
   - consideration of how much he has changed and, if not, whether it matters.

7. ***A Taste of Honey***

   Your response might have included some of the following points:
   - Jo seems unconcerned about how she will manage as Geof questions her about money
   - she shows immaturity and lack of understanding of what motherhood will mean
   - her attitude might be a way of avoiding her true feelings
   - she does not say she wants to be a mother but refuses to consider an abortion
   - she says she does not know much about love so the audience may wonder whether she could love the baby
   - Geof, not knowing Helen, assumes that she will care because she is Jo's mother
   - later she panics and says 'I don't want to be a mother'
   - Geof tries to help her but she reacts by joking and flirting, trying to avoid the subject

- Helen's idea of motherhood is unconventional
- she is selfish and shows little concern for Jo
- she becomes sentimental about the baby but focuses on material things like the cot
- their love–hate relationship is the central one in both their lives.

8. *An Inspector Calls*

   Your response might have included some of the following points:
   - the Inspector takes charge and commands respect
   - he is an outsider and does not belong to the world the Birlings live in
   - he acts like a detective in that he is investigating something and questioning people
   - he is not really investigating a crime but is looking into the reasons for Eva's act
   - he apportions blame and judges the other characters
   - he moralises about society and warns of the consequences of behaving like the Birlings
   - his name, Goole, is pronounced in the same way as 'ghoul' – is he a ghost from the future?
   - he has come from the 1940s, when the play was written, to examine an earlier time
   - he may be warning the audience not to return to the society of 1912
   - he can be seen as the voice of the writer.

9. *The History Boys*

   Your response might have included some of the following points:
   - Mrs Lintott asks if Irwin has 'ceased to be a teacher and become a friend', implying that it is impossible to be both
   - Posner is looking for personal advice, which could be seen as part of a teacher's job
   - Irwin seeks to discover more about Hector's relationship with boys
   - this could be seen as crossing a line and/or showing concern about Hector crossing lines
   - Posner notices Irwin's interest in Dakin
   - Dakin takes advantage of this interest and treats Irwin as if he were a friend
   - Hector blurs the lines between teacher/pupil relationships and friendships
   - even without the 'groping' he could be seen as over-friendly
   - it could be said that a 'friendly' relationship with pupils is helpful in teaching but that is not the same as being friends
   - at times the friendships between staff and pupils can appear to be fun and positive, but it can also be harmful and manipulative (on both sides).

10. *Blood Brothers*

    Your response might have included some of the following points:
    - she stands up for Mickey to his brother and other older children
    - she is one of the gang, equal to the boys in their games
    - she is protective and caring towards Mickey
    - the conversation about dying prefigures the end of the play, as does Sammy's gun
    - she is pragmatic in a comic, childish way ('if y'dead, there's no school')
    - in the extract Mickey introduces her to Edward for the first time – their relationship will be crucial
    - in the park Linda proves better than the boys at shooting – is Russell making a feminist point?
    - she is outgoing and witty, helping to create a lighter atmosphere as she and the boys have fun together
    - she is in love with Mickey but, as his wife, she is frustrated in her attempts to help him
    - she turns to Edward for help, unwittingly bringing the tragedy closer.

Section B: 19th Century Prose

Pages 40–45

Questions 11–16

Use the table below to mark your response out of 40.

See below the table for suggested content that you might have included or discussed for each question.

Marks	Skills
33–40 (Grades 8–9)	• You have sustained focus on the task, including overview, conveying ideas with consistent coherence in an appropriate register. • You have taken a sensitive and evaluative approach to the task and analysed the text critically. • You have shown a perceptive understanding of the text, engaging fully, perhaps with some originality in your personal response. • Your response includes pertinent direct references to the text, including quotations. • You have analysed and appreciated the writer's use of language, form and structure. • You have made assured reference to meaning and effects, exploring and evaluating the way meaning and ideas are conveyed through language, structure and form. • You have used precise subject terminology in an appropriate context. • You have shown an assured understanding of the relationship between texts and the contexts in which they were written, including (where relevant) those of period, location, social structures and literary contexts such as genre. • You have shown assured understanding of contexts in which texts are engaged with by different audiences.
25–32 (Grades 6–7)	• You have sustained focus on the task, conveying ideas with consistent coherence in an appropriate register. • You have taken a thoughtful approach to the task. • You have shown a secure understanding of key aspects of the text, with considerable engagement. • Your response includes well-chosen direct references to the text, including quotations. • You have discussed and increasingly analysed the writer's use of language, form and structure. • You have made thoughtful reference to the meaning and effects of stylistic features used by the writer. • You have used apt subject terminology. • You have shown secure understanding of the relationship between texts and the contexts in which they were written, including (where relevant) those of period, location, social structures and literary contexts such as genre. • You have shown secure understanding of contexts in which texts are engaged with by different audiences.

17–24 (Grades 4–5)	<ul><li>You have focused on the task, conveying ideas with general coherence usually in an appropriate register.</li><li>You have taken a straightforward approach to the task.</li><li>You have shown understanding of key aspects of the text, with engagement.</li><li>Your response includes appropriate direct references to the text, including quotations.</li><li>You have commented on and begun to analyse the writer's use of language, form and structure.</li><li>You have made some reference to meaning and effects.</li><li>You have used relevant subject terminology.</li><li>You have shown understanding of the relationship between texts and the contexts in which they were written, including (where relevant) those of period, location, social structures and literary contexts such as genre.</li><li>You have shown understanding of contexts in which texts are engaged with by different audiences.</li></ul>
9–16 (Grades 2–3)	<ul><li>You have shown some focus on the task, conveying ideas with some coherence, sometimes in an appropriate register.</li><li>You have taken a limited approach to the task.</li><li>You have shown some understanding of key aspects of the text, with some engagement.</li><li>Your response includes some direct references to the text, including some quotations.</li><li>You have recognised and made simple comments on the writer's use of language, form and structure.</li><li>You may have made limited reference to meaning and effects.</li><li>You may have used some relevant subject terminology.</li><li>You have shown some understanding of the relationship between texts and the contexts in which they were written, including (where relevant) those of period, location, social structures and literary contexts such as genre.</li><li>You have shown some understanding of contexts in which texts are engaged with by different audiences.</li></ul>
1–8 (U–Grade 1)	<ul><li>You have shown limited focus on the task, conveying ideas with occasional coherence, sometimes in an appropriate register.</li><li>You have taken a simple approach to the task.</li><li>You have shown a basic understanding of some key aspects of the text, with a little engagement.</li><li>Your response includes some general reference to the text, perhaps including some quotations.</li><li>You have made generalised comments on the writer's use of language, form and structure.</li><li>You may have made basic reference to meaning and effects.</li><li>You may have used some subject terminology but not always accurately.</li><li>You have shown limited understanding of the relationship between texts and the contexts in which they were written, including (where relevant) those of period, location, social structures and literary contexts such as genre.</li><li>You have shown limited understanding of contexts in which texts are engaged with by different audiences.</li></ul>

11. *A Christmas Carol*

Your response might have included some of the following points:

- Scrooge is reluctant to go with this Spirit but is less aggressive and uncooperative than before
- the ghost is gentle but firm
- the symbolism of light
- the ghost reassures him that he has come to help but Scrooge is nervous
- when the darkness vanishes it is 'a clear, cold, winter day' suggesting Scrooge will see more clearly
- Dickens uses these scenes to show how Scrooge has changed psychologically, his behaviour the result of nurture, not nature
- how his lack of love as a child and the death of Fan explain his coldness and his attitude to his nephew
- the cumulative effect of the bad choices he sees himself making
- the sense of what he might have been had he not worshipped money – an employer like Fezziwig or part of a family like Belle or the Cratchits
- the scenes he witnesses make Scrooge start to realise he can change for the better
- the context of Christian ideas and morality
- the context of the norms of Victorian family life
- the literary genre of the ghost story.

12. *Silas Marner*

Your response might have included some of the following points:

- he has had no relationship with Eppie until now
- Eppie considers Silas to be her father
- Godfrey says very little in response to Eppie's rejection of him: his feelings are implied rather than stated
- he is frustrated in his desire to put things right
- Nancy speaks on his behalf, saying that Eppie has a 'duty' to her 'lawful' father
- Nancy supports and helps him despite his previous actions, showing a strong love between them
- Nancy's reactions are informed by her mourning for her own child and her desire to be a mother
- throughout the novel he is portrayed as a good man and a good husband, haunted by his secret past
- he is conscious of how he failed Eppie and her mother
- his first marriage is seen as a mistake and his second as a success, but he cannot escape his past failings
- at the end he accepts Eppie's decision and the novel ends with a feeling that he and Nancy have learned to live with it
- context of 19th century ideas about marriage and family life
- context of Christian morality and practice
- consciousness of social class.

13. *Pride and Prejudice*

Your response might have included some of the following points:

- extreme contrast in the reactions of Mr and Mrs Bennet
- Mrs Bennet disappointed because she saw Mr Collins as a good match for Elizabeth
- although expressed in a comical way, getting her daughters married is a serious business
- Mr Bennet's 'tranquil' response seems more reasonable but reflects his refusal to take his wife's concerns seriously
- seeing Charlotte as more foolish than his daughter is ironic as, in fact, Charlotte's decision is sensible and practical
- both parents have favourites – Mr Bennet favours Elizabeth
- as a father, Mr Bennet is loving (at least to Elizabeth) but rather distant and selfish
- Mrs Bennet is overbearing and embarrassing but sees herself as working for her daughters' happiness

- context of the girls' social and economic circumstances – they are dependent on their father and future husbands.

14. War of the Worlds

Your response might have included some of the following points:

- the extract starts by directly addressing the reader, anxious to get the message across
- use of extended metaphor of water
- precision about times and places as if writing a report
- describes the violence caused by panic
- there is no organisation or control
- in the extract, people are not given names or distinguished from each other but elsewhere individuals' stories are told
- the narrator reports his own and others' experiences, especially those of his brother
- shows how panic brings out the worst in people but also some good as some people try to help each other
- the narrator's account of his own experiences shows him to be more thoughtful than most, planning his actions carefully and not panicking
- context of the science fiction genre, and ideas about advances in science
- the use of the familiar and everyday as a setting for extraordinary events.

15. Jane Eyre

Your response might have included some of the following points:

- Jane is included in the party but sits apart, listening
- she slips away by a side door, wanting to be as unobtrusive as possible
- Rochester seems concerned but questions her abruptly
- his use of imperatives as he gives her orders
- she is conscious of not having the 'freedom' to speak to him as an equal
- she is from an upper or upper-middle class background but is impoverished and has to earn her living
- her position means that she can mix with and observe servants as well as employers and their friends
- she does not like the affectations of snobbish people like the Ingrams
- her judgements are not based on class
- Rochester does not care about her class or background
- ultimately she returns to her 'proper' position in life, receiving an inheritance and making a 'good' marriage.

16. The Strange Case of Dr Jekyll and Mr Hyde

Your response might have included some of the following points:

- the description of the scene at twilight creates a sad and gentle mood
- Jekyll is compared to a 'disconsolate prisoner', making him seem like a victim
- Jekyll's words about being 'low' and 'it will not be long' suggest an illness he is not in control of
- he is polite and pleasant when talking to the other men
- the sudden change in his look is frightening and his 'terror and despair' suggest a victim
- Utterson and Lanyon characterise him as someone who used to be a good, reasonable man but has become strange
- Jekyll's friends see him as a victim of Hyde and want to help him
- Dr Lanyon's narrative reveals the full horror of Jekyll's 'moral turpitude'
- Jekyll's own narrative gives insight into his motives and his feelings about what he has done, making him sympathetic again
- consideration of Gothic tradition and the horror genre
- context of scientific discovery and ethical questions
- context of growing interest in psychology.

Section C: Unseen Poetry

Pages 46–47

Question 17

Use the table below to mark your response. Mark part **(a)** first (out of 15) and then part **(b)** (out of 25).

See below the table for suggested content that you might have included or discussed for each question.

Marks	Skills
(a) 13–15 **(b) 21–25** **(Grades 8–9)**	• You have sustained focus on the task, including overview, conveying ideas with consistent coherence in an appropriate register. • You have taken a sensitive and evaluative approach to the task and analysed the text critically. • You have shown a perceptive understanding of the text, engaging fully, perhaps with some originality, in your personal response. • Your response includes pertinent direct references to the text, including quotations. • You have analysed and appreciated the writers' use of language, form and structure. • You have made assured reference to meaning and effects, exploring and evaluating the way meaning and ideas are conveyed through language, structure and form. • You have used precise subject terminology in an appropriate context. • You have shown an assured understanding of the relationship between texts and the contexts in which they were written, including (where relevant) those of period, location, social structures and literary contexts such as genre. • You have shown assured understanding of contexts in which texts are engaged with by different audiences. **Part (b) only:** • Your comparison is critical, illuminating and sustained. • You have discussed a wide range of similarities and differences between the poems.
(a) 10–12 **(b) 16–20** **(Grades 6–7)**	• You have sustained focus on the task, conveying ideas with consistent coherence in an appropriate register. • You have taken a thoughtful approach to the task. • You have shown a secure understanding of key aspects of the text, with considerable engagement. • Your response includes well-chosen direct references to the text, including quotations. • You have discussed and increasingly analysed the writers' use of language, form and structure. • You have made thoughtful reference to the meaning and effects of stylistic features used by the writer. • You have used apt subject terminology.

		• You have shown secure understanding of the relationship between texts and the contexts in which they were written, including (where relevant) those of period, location, social structures and literary contexts such as genre. • You have shown secure understanding of contexts in which texts are engaged with by different audiences. **Part (b) only:** • Your comparison is focused, coherent and sustained. • You have clearly discussed the similarities and differences between the poems.
(a) 7–9 (b) 11–15 (Grades 4–5)		• You have focused on the task, conveying ideas with general coherence usually in an appropriate register. • You have taken a straightforward approach to the task. • You have shown understanding of key aspects of the text, with engagement. • Your response includes appropriate direct references to the text, including quotations. • You have commented on, and begun to analyse, the writers' use of language, form and structure. • You have made some reference to meaning and effects. • You have used relevant subject terminology. • You have shown understanding of the relationship between texts and the contexts in which they were written, including (where relevant) those of period, location, social structures and literary contexts such as genre. • You have shown understanding of contexts in which texts are engaged with by different audiences. **Part (b) only:** • Your comparison is focused. • You have discussed some valid similarities and differences between the poems.
(a) 4–6 (b) 6–10 (Grades 2–3)		• You have shown some focus on the task, conveying ideas with some coherence, sometimes in an appropriate register. • You have taken a limited approach to the task. • You have shown some understanding of key aspects of the text, with some engagement. • Your response includes some direct references to the text, including some quotations. • You have recognised and made simple comments on the writers' use of language, form and structure. • You may have made limited reference to meaning and effects. • You may have used some relevant subject terminology. • You have shown some understanding of the relationship between texts and the contexts in which they were written, including (where relevant) those of period, location, social structures and literary contexts such as genre. • You have shown some understanding of contexts in which texts are engaged with by different audiences. **Part (b) only:** • Your comparison is general. • You have discussed the obvious similarities and differences between the poems.
(a) 1–3 (b) 1–5 (U–Grade 1)		• You have shown limited focus on the task, conveying ideas with occasional coherence, sometimes in an appropriate register. • You have taken a simple approach to the task. • You have shown a basic understanding of some key aspects of the text, with a little engagement. • Your response includes some general reference to the text, perhaps including some quotations. • You have made generalised comments on the writers' use of language, form and structure. • You may have made basic reference to meaning and effects. • You may have used some subject terminology but not always accurately. • You have shown limited understanding of the relationship between texts and the contexts in which they were written, including (where relevant) those of period, location, social structures and literary contexts such as genre. • You have shown limited understanding of contexts in which texts are engaged with by different audiences. **Part (b) only:** • Your comparison is very limited. • You may have shown basic awareness of the obvious similarities and differences between the poems.

17. (a) **Your response might have included some of the following points:**
    - the repetition of 'I remember, I remember' at the beginning of each stanza (anaphora)
    - short lines and rhyme give a childish feel to the poem
    - words like 'little' and 'peeping' add to a sentimental view of childhood
    - the memories all involve literal imagery in the description of nature
    - he looks back on childhood as a time of pure happiness
    - each stanza contrasts a happy memory with his current feelings
    - childhood is seen from the point of view of an older, sicker person
    - there is a lot of colour in the second stanza and movement in the third, giving a sense of a child's wonder and enthusiasm
    - the regular metre and rhyme scheme contain his emotions, both joyful and sad
    - the last four lines almost dismiss childhood experience ('It was a childish ignorance') and reflect on how he has changed
    - he does not explain why he thinks he is 'farther off from Heaven' and makes the reader wonder about the kind of life he has led.

17. (b) **Your response might have included some of the following points:**
    - the first poem is written by an older man looking back on childhood; the second is from a child's point of view
    - when describing childhood experience, both express joy and excitement, both focusing on a swing
    - both describe nature (literal imagery)
    - both seem to have safe, secure childhoods, contained in gardens
    - Stevenson's poem, unlike Hood's, shows no awareness of growing old or mortality
    - Stevenson's poem has a simple rhyme scheme and metre, like Hood's, but has shorter stanzas
    - Stevenson's sentiments are as simple as his form, unlike Hood's
    - Stevenson's poem might have been written for children.